50 Japan Winter Holiday Recipes for Home

By: Kelly Johnson

Table of Contents

- Sukiyaki
- Shabu-Shabu
- Oden
- Chanko Nabe
- Kakuni (Braised Pork Belly)
- Mochi Soup (Zoni)
- Yudofu (Tofu Hot Pot)
- Tempura Udon
- Miso Ramen
- Soba Noodles with Tempura
- Katsu Curry
- Nabe Yaki Udon
- Hot Pot with Seafoods
- Japanese Curry Rice
- Tori Kotsu Ramen
- Tonkotsu Ramen
- Chicken and Mushroom Stew
- Grilled Daikon
- Oyakodon (Chicken and Egg Rice Bowl)
- Umeboshi and Pork Rice
- Miso Soup with Clams
- Salmon and Vegetable Nabe
- Pork Shogayaki
- Sukiyaki Udon
- Buta no Kakuni (Braised Pork Belly)
- Japanese Beef Stew
- Yaki Onigiri (Grilled Rice Balls)
- Japanese Meatballs (Tsukune)
- Miso-Glazed Eggplant
- Sweet Potato Tempura
- Chicken Teriyaki
- Shrimp Tempura

- Beef and Vegetable Stir-Fry
- Japanese-Style Lasagna
- Japanese Potatoes and Beef
- Pork and Daikon Radish Stew
- Simmered Kabocha Squash
- Tofu and Vegetable Stir-Fry
- Salmon and Cabbage Stew
- Nabeyaki Ramen
- Braised Chicken with Shiitake Mushrooms
- Japanese Style Stuffed Peppers
- Miso-Glazed Chicken Wings
- Hot and Sour Udon Soup
- Tempura Soba Noodles
- Korean-Style Spicy Tofu Stew
- Sweet Potato and Pork Stew
- Miso Cod Fish
- Niku Jaga (Beef and Potato Stew)
- Spicy Tuna Pizza

Sukiyaki

Ingredients:

- **For the Broth:**
    - 1/2 cup soy sauce
    - 1/2 cup mirin (sweet rice wine)
    - 1/4 cup sake (Japanese rice wine)
    - 1/4 cup sugar
    - 1 cup dashi stock (or substitute with beef or vegetable broth)
- **For the Sukiyaki:**
    - 1 lb (450g) thinly sliced beef (ribeye or sirloin works well)
    - 1 block of tofu, cut into cubes
    - 1 onion, thinly sliced
    - 2-3 cups mushrooms (shiitake, enoki, or button mushrooms), trimmed
    - 1-2 cups napa cabbage, chopped
    - 1-2 cups spinach or other leafy greens
    - 1 cup shirataki noodles (konjac noodles) or udon noodles
    - 2-3 green onions, cut into 1-inch pieces
    - 1-2 carrots, thinly sliced (optional)
- **For Serving:**
    - Cooked rice
    - Raw eggs (optional, for dipping)

Instructions:

1. **Prepare the Broth:**
    1. **Combine Ingredients**: In a bowl, mix together the soy sauce, mirin, sake, sugar, and dashi stock. Stir until the sugar is dissolved.
2. **Prepare the Ingredients:**
    1. **Slice Beef**: If not pre-sliced, slice the beef thinly against the grain.
    2. **Prepare Vegetables**: Slice the onion, chop the cabbage, and cut the tofu into cubes. Trim the mushrooms and slice the carrots if using.
    3. **Prepare Noodles**: If using shirataki noodles, rinse them under cold water and drain. For udon noodles, cook according to package instructions.
3. **Cook the Sukiyaki:**
    1. **Heat the Pot**: In a large skillet or sukiyaki pot, heat a small amount of oil over medium heat.
    2. **Brown the Beef**: Add a few slices of beef to the pot and cook until browned. Remove and set aside. Repeat with the remaining beef.
    3. **Cook Vegetables and Tofu**: In the same pot, add the onion, tofu, and mushrooms. Cook for a few minutes until the vegetables start to soften.
    4. **Add Broth**: Pour the prepared broth into the pot, bringing it to a simmer.

5. **Add Noodles and Greens**: Add the shirataki or udon noodles, cabbage, spinach, and green onions. Simmer until the vegetables are tender and the noodles are heated through.
4. **Serve**:
    1. **Serve Hot**: Ladle the hot pot ingredients into bowls.
    2. **Optional**: If desired, serve with raw eggs for dipping. To use, crack an egg into a small bowl and use it as a dipping sauce for the cooked beef and vegetables.
    3. **Accompaniments**: Serve with steamed rice on the side.

Tips:

- **Beef**: Thinly sliced beef is essential for sukiyaki. You can find pre-sliced beef at Asian grocery stores, or slice it yourself if it's partially frozen.
- **Broth**: Adjust the sweetness and saltiness of the broth according to your taste. You can add more sugar or soy sauce if needed.
- **Vegetables**: Feel free to customize the vegetables based on your preferences or seasonal availability.

Sukiyaki is a flavorful and interactive dish that brings warmth and comfort during the colder months. Enjoy this communal meal with family and friends!

Shabu-Shabu

Ingredients:

- **For the Broth**:
    - 6 cups dashi stock (or substitute with chicken or vegetable broth)
    - 2-3 slices of kombu (dried kelp), optional for extra flavor
    - 1-2 tablespoons soy sauce (optional, for added flavor)
- **For the Hot Pot**:
    - 1 lb (450g) thinly sliced beef (ribeye or sirloin works well)
    - 1 block of tofu, cut into cubes
    - 2 cups mushrooms (shiitake, enoki, or button mushrooms), trimmed
    - 2 cups napa cabbage, chopped
    - 1-2 cups spinach or other leafy greens
    - 1-2 carrots, thinly sliced
    - 1 cup sliced green onions
    - 1-2 cups udon noodles or rice (for serving)
- **For Dipping Sauces**:
    - **Ponzu Sauce**:
        - 1/4 cup soy sauce
        - 1/4 cup lemon or lime juice
        - 1 tablespoon mirin (sweet rice wine)
        - 1 tablespoon rice vinegar
    - **Sesame Sauce**:
        - 1/4 cup tahini (or sesame paste)
        - 2 tablespoons soy sauce
        - 1 tablespoon sugar
        - 1 tablespoon rice vinegar
        - 1 tablespoon water (adjust for consistency)
- **Garnishes** (optional):
    - Chopped scallions
    - Grated daikon radish
    - Sesame seeds
    - Chopped cilantro

Instructions:

1. **Prepare the Broth**:
    1. **Combine Ingredients**: In a large pot, add the dashi stock and kombu slices if using. Bring to a simmer over medium heat. Remove the kombu just before the broth starts boiling.
    2. **Add Soy Sauce**: Add soy sauce to taste if desired. Keep the broth hot but not boiling.

2. **Prepare the Ingredients**:
    1. **Slice Beef**: Thinly slice the beef if not pre-sliced. Frozen beef is easier to slice thinly.
    2. **Prepare Vegetables and Tofu**: Cut the tofu into cubes, slice the mushrooms, chop the cabbage, and slice the carrots. Prepare any additional vegetables you like.
3. **Cook the Hot Pot**:
    1. **Heat the Pot**: Place the pot with broth on a portable burner at the table.
    2. **Add Ingredients**: Add vegetables, tofu, and noodles (if using) to the pot. Let them cook briefly until tender.
    3. **Cook Beef**: Using chopsticks or a ladle, dip the thinly sliced beef into the boiling broth. Swirl it around for a few seconds until cooked through. The beef cooks very quickly.
4. **Prepare Dipping Sauces**:
    1. **Mix Ponzu Sauce**: Combine soy sauce, lemon or lime juice, mirin, and rice vinegar in a small bowl. Mix well.
    2. **Mix Sesame Sauce**: Combine tahini, soy sauce, sugar, rice vinegar, and water in a bowl. Adjust the consistency with water if needed.
5. **Serve**:
    1. **Dipping**: Dip the cooked beef and vegetables into the dipping sauces and enjoy.
    2. **Accompaniments**: Serve the Shabu-Shabu with steamed rice or noodles and garnishes like chopped scallions, grated daikon, sesame seeds, and cilantro.

Tips:

- **Beef**: Thinly sliced beef is key to Shabu-Shabu. You can find pre-sliced beef at Asian grocery stores or slice it yourself if partially frozen.
- **Broth**: Keep the broth hot throughout the meal to ensure ingredients cook quickly.
- **Interactive Meal**: Shabu-Shabu is meant to be a communal and interactive dining experience. Cook and dip ingredients at the table for a fun, social meal.

Shabu-Shabu is a delicious and customizable dish that's perfect for winter gatherings. Enjoy the interactive nature of cooking and dipping your ingredients right at the table!

Oden

Ingredients:

- **For the Broth**:
    - 6 cups dashi stock (or substitute with chicken or vegetable broth)
    - 1/4 cup soy sauce
    - 1/4 cup mirin (sweet rice wine)
    - 2 tablespoons sake (Japanese rice wine)
    - 1 tablespoon sugar
- **For the Oden**:
    - 1 large daikon radish, peeled and cut into rounds
    - 4-6 eggs, peeled (boil and peel them beforehand)
    - 1 block of tofu, cut into cubes (firm tofu is best)
    - 1 package of konnyaku (konjac) noodles or slices, cut into pieces
    - 1-2 packs of various fish cakes (e.g., chikuwa, oden-age, hanpen)
    - 1-2 sheets of kombu (dried kelp), cut into pieces
    - 1-2 pieces of grilled or boiled sausage (optional, for extra flavor)
- **For Garnish and Serving**:
    - Mustard (karashi) for dipping
    - Pickled vegetables (optional)

Instructions:

1. **Prepare the Broth**:
    1. **Combine Ingredients**: In a large pot, combine the dashi stock, soy sauce, mirin, sake, and sugar.
    2. **Simmer**: Bring to a gentle simmer over medium heat, stirring occasionally until the sugar is dissolved. Adjust seasoning to taste.
2. **Prepare the Ingredients**:
    1. **Daikon**: Peel and cut the daikon radish into 1-inch thick rounds. Blanch them in boiling water for 2-3 minutes to remove bitterness, then drain.
    2. **Eggs**: Boil the eggs for about 7 minutes, then peel and set aside.
    3. **Tofu**: Cut the tofu into bite-sized cubes.
    4. **Konnyaku**: If using konnyaku, cut it into bite-sized pieces and blanch briefly in boiling water to remove its unique smell.
    5. **Fish Cakes**: Cut fish cakes into bite-sized pieces if needed.
    6. **Kombu**: If using kombu, cut it into pieces. It adds umami to the broth.
3. **Cook the Oden**:
    1. **Add Ingredients**: Add the daikon, eggs, tofu, konnyaku, fish cakes, and kombu to the pot with the broth.

2. **Simmer**: Bring to a gentle simmer over medium heat. Cook for at least 30 minutes, or until the daikon is tender and the flavors are well combined. The longer it simmers, the more flavorful it becomes.
4. **Serve**:
    1. **Ladle into Bowls**: Serve the Oden hot, ladling the ingredients and broth into bowls.
    2. **Garnish**: Provide mustard (karashi) on the side for dipping. Pickled vegetables can also be served on the side if desired.

Tips:

- **Ingredients**: Oden is very flexible. You can add other ingredients such as mushrooms, meatballs, or different types of fish cakes based on your preferences.
- **Broth**: The broth can be adjusted to taste. If you prefer a richer flavor, add more soy sauce or mirin.
- **Make Ahead**: Oden tastes even better the next day as the flavors continue to develop. It can be stored in the refrigerator and reheated.

Oden is a hearty and warming dish, perfect for gathering around on a cold day. Enjoy this comforting Japanese stew with friends and family!

Chanko Nabe

Ingredients:

- **For the Broth**:
    - 6 cups dashi stock (or substitute with chicken or vegetable broth)
    - 1/4 cup soy sauce
    - 1/4 cup mirin (sweet rice wine)
    - 2 tablespoons sake (Japanese rice wine)
    - 1 tablespoon sugar
- **For the Hot Pot**:
    - 1 lb (450g) chicken thighs or drumsticks, cut into chunks
    - 1/2 lb (225g) pork belly or pork shoulder, sliced into thin strips
    - 1 block of tofu, cut into cubes (firm tofu works well)
    - 1 large daikon radish, peeled and sliced into rounds
    - 2-3 cups napa cabbage, chopped
    - 1-2 cups mushrooms (shiitake, enoki, or button mushrooms), trimmed
    - 1-2 carrots, sliced
    - 1 cup sliced green onions
    - 1 cup udon noodles or cooked rice (for serving)
    - 1-2 tablespoons vegetable oil
- **For Garnish and Serving**:
    - Soy sauce or additional seasoning (to taste)
    - Fresh parsley or chopped scallions (optional)
    - Sesame seeds (optional)

Instructions:

1. **Prepare the Broth**:
    1. **Combine Ingredients**: In a large pot, combine the dashi stock, soy sauce, mirin, sake, and sugar.
    2. **Simmer**: Bring to a gentle simmer over medium heat, stirring occasionally until the sugar is dissolved. Adjust seasoning to taste.
2. **Prepare the Ingredients**:
    1. **Cook Meats**: Heat a small amount of vegetable oil in a skillet over medium heat. Add the chicken and pork and cook until lightly browned. Remove and set aside.
    2. **Prepare Vegetables**: Slice the daikon radish, chop the cabbage, slice the carrots, and trim the mushrooms. Cut the tofu into cubes.
3. **Cook the Hot Pot**:
    1. **Combine Ingredients**: Add the browned chicken and pork to the pot with the broth. Bring to a simmer.
    2. **Add Vegetables**: Add the daikon radish, carrots, and mushrooms to the pot. Simmer until the vegetables are tender.

3. **Add Tofu and Greens**: Add the tofu and napa cabbage. Simmer for an additional 5-10 minutes until the tofu is heated through and the cabbage is wilted.
4. **Add Noodles or Rice**: If using udon noodles, add them to the pot and cook until heated through. If using rice, you can serve it on the side or add it directly to the pot before serving.

4. **Serve**:
    1. **Ladle into Bowls**: Serve the hot pot directly from the pot to bowls, making sure to include a variety of meats and vegetables in each serving.
    2. **Garnish**: Garnish with fresh parsley or scallions if desired. Sprinkle with sesame seeds for extra flavor.

Tips:

- **Meats**: You can also use other meats such as beef or seafood based on your preference.
- **Broth**: Adjust the seasoning of the broth to your taste. If you prefer a stronger flavor, add more soy sauce or mirin.
- **Vegetables**: Feel free to customize the vegetables according to what's in season or what you prefer.

Chanko Nabe is a versatile and filling dish, perfect for sharing with family and friends. Enjoy this comforting Japanese hot pot as a warm and hearty meal during the colder months!

Kakuni (Braised Pork Belly)

Ingredients:

- **For the Braise:**
    - 1 lb (450g) pork belly, cut into 2-inch cubes
    - 2 tablespoons vegetable oil
    - 1 large onion, sliced
    - 4-5 cloves garlic, minced
    - 1-inch piece of ginger, sliced
    - 1/2 cup soy sauce
    - 1/4 cup mirin (sweet rice wine)
    - 1/4 cup sake (Japanese rice wine)
    - 1/4 cup sugar (brown sugar or white sugar)
    - 2 cups water or dashi stock
    - 2-3 green onions, cut into 2-inch pieces (optional)
    - 2-3 pieces of star anise (optional)
    - 2 tablespoons rice vinegar (optional, for a touch of acidity)
- **For Garnish (optional):**
    - Chopped green onions
    - Sesame seeds

Instructions:

1. **Prepare the Pork Belly:**
    1. **Blanch the Pork:** Bring a large pot of water to a boil. Add the pork belly cubes and blanch for 2-3 minutes to remove impurities. Drain and rinse under cold water.
2. **Sear the Pork Belly:**
    1. **Heat Oil:** In a large pot or Dutch oven, heat the vegetable oil over medium-high heat.
    2. **Brown Pork:** Add the pork belly cubes and sear on all sides until browned. Remove the pork belly from the pot and set aside.
3. **Prepare the Braise:**
    1. **Sauté Aromatics:** In the same pot, add the sliced onion, garlic, and ginger. Sauté for a few minutes until the onions are softened and fragrant.
    2. **Add Liquids and Seasonings:** Return the pork belly to the pot. Add the soy sauce, mirin, sake, sugar, and water or dashi stock. Stir to combine.
    3. **Add Optional Ingredients:** If using, add the green onions, star anise, and rice vinegar. Stir to mix.
4. **Braise the Pork:**
    1. **Simmer:** Bring the mixture to a boil, then reduce the heat to low. Cover and let it simmer for 1.5 to 2 hours, or until the pork belly is tender and the sauce has

thickened. Check occasionally and add a bit more water if needed to keep the pork covered.

5. **Reduce the Sauce**:
    1. **Uncover and Reduce**: Once the pork is tender, uncover the pot and increase the heat slightly. Let the sauce reduce and thicken to your desired consistency. Stir occasionally.
6. **Serve**:
    1. **Garnish**: Transfer the pork belly to a serving plate or bowl. Spoon some of the braising liquid over the top.
    2. **Optional Garnishes**: Garnish with chopped green onions and sesame seeds if desired.
    3. **Accompaniments**: Serve Kakuni with steamed rice and pickled vegetables for a complete meal.

Tips:

- **Pork Belly**: Choose pork belly with a good balance of meat and fat for the best texture and flavor.
- **Braising Liquid**: Adjust the sweetness and saltiness of the braising liquid to your taste. You can add more sugar or soy sauce if desired.
- **Make Ahead**: Kakuni can be made ahead of time and tastes even better the next day as the flavors continue to develop.

Kakuni is a rich and comforting dish that showcases the deliciousness of braised pork belly. Enjoy this flavorful Japanese classic with family and friends!

Mochi Soup (Zoni)

Ingredients:

- **For the Broth**:
    - 4 cups dashi stock (you can make dashi from scratch or use instant dashi powder)
    - 1/4 cup soy sauce
    - 1/4 cup mirin (sweet rice wine)
    - 1 tablespoon sake (Japanese rice wine)
    - 1-2 tablespoons sugar (optional, adjust to taste)
- **For the Soup**:
    - 4-6 pieces of mochi (glutinous rice cakes), cut into 1-2 inch squares
    - 1 cup sliced shiitake mushrooms (or other mushrooms of your choice)
    - 1 cup sliced carrots
    - 1 cup chopped spinach or other leafy greens
    - 1/2 cup sliced green onions
    - 1/2 cup sliced daikon radish (optional)
    - 1/2 cup cooked chicken, pork, or shrimp (optional, for added protein)
    - 1 tablespoon vegetable oil (for sautéing)
- **For Garnish (optional)**:
    - Chopped fresh parsley or cilantro
    - Pickled vegetables
    - Seaweed (nori), cut into strips

Instructions:

1. **Prepare the Broth**:
    1. **Combine Ingredients**: In a large pot, combine the dashi stock, soy sauce, mirin, sake, and sugar if using.
    2. **Simmer**: Bring to a gentle simmer over medium heat, stirring occasionally. Adjust the seasoning to taste.
2. **Prepare the Soup Ingredients**:
    1. **Cook Vegetables**: Heat a tablespoon of vegetable oil in a skillet over medium heat. Sauté the mushrooms, carrots, and daikon radish until slightly tender. Set aside.
    2. **Cook Protein**: If using chicken, pork, or shrimp, cook them in the same skillet until fully cooked. Set aside.
3. **Cook the Mochi**:
    1. **Grill or Pan-Fry**: To achieve a crispy exterior, grill or pan-fry the mochi pieces until golden and slightly crispy on the outside. Alternatively, you can directly add them to the soup without pre-cooking, but grilling gives a nice texture.
4. **Combine and Simmer**:

1. **Add Ingredients**: Add the sautéed vegetables and protein to the pot with the broth.
   2. **Simmer**: Gently add the mochi pieces to the broth. Simmer for 5-10 minutes until the mochi is soft and has absorbed some of the broth's flavor.
5. **Add Greens**:
   1. **Finish**: Add the chopped spinach or other leafy greens just a minute or two before serving, allowing them to wilt but not overcook.
6. **Serve**:
   1. **Ladle into Bowls**: Serve the Zoni hot, ladling the soup, mochi, and vegetables into bowls.
   2. **Garnish**: Garnish with chopped parsley or cilantro, pickled vegetables, and seaweed strips if desired.

Tips:

- **Mochi**: Make sure to cook the mochi pieces thoroughly so they are soft and chewy. If using leftover mochi, you may need to simmer them longer to soften.
- **Broth**: Adjust the seasoning of the broth to suit your taste. You can add more soy sauce or mirin if you prefer a stronger flavor.
- **Vegetables**: Feel free to customize the vegetables based on what you have available or what you prefer.

Mochi Soup (Zoni) is a comforting and flavorful dish that captures the essence of Japanese New Year's celebrations. Enjoy this warming soup as a special treat during the winter season!

Yudofu (Tofu Hot Pot)

Ingredients:

- **For the Broth**:
    - 4 cups dashi stock (you can make dashi from scratch or use instant dashi powder)
    - 2 tablespoons soy sauce
    - 2 tablespoons mirin (sweet rice wine)
    - 1 tablespoon sake (Japanese rice wine)
    - 1 teaspoon salt (adjust to taste)
- **For the Hot Pot**:
    - 1 block of firm or extra-firm tofu, cut into large cubes
    - 1 cup sliced shiitake mushrooms or other mushrooms of your choice
    - 1 cup chopped leafy greens (e.g., spinach, bok choy, or napa cabbage)
    - 1/2 cup sliced green onions
    - 1 small daikon radish, peeled and sliced (optional)
    - 1 small carrot, peeled and sliced (optional)
- **For Dipping Sauces** (optional):
    - **Ponzu Sauce**: A citrus-based soy sauce, often served with a bit of grated daikon radish.
    - **Goma-dare (Sesame Sauce)**: A rich, nutty sauce made from sesame paste, soy sauce, and other seasonings.

Instructions:

1. **Prepare the Broth**:
    1. **Combine Ingredients**: In a large pot, combine the dashi stock, soy sauce, mirin, sake, and salt.
    2. **Simmer**: Bring the mixture to a gentle simmer over medium heat. Adjust seasoning to taste.
2. **Prepare the Ingredients**:
    1. **Cut Tofu**: Cut the tofu into large, bite-sized cubes.
    2. **Prepare Vegetables**: Slice the mushrooms, chop the greens, and slice the daikon radish and carrot if using.
3. **Cook the Yudofu**:
    1. **Add Ingredients**: Gently add the tofu cubes and any vegetables (except leafy greens) to the simmering broth.
    2. **Simmer**: Simmer gently for 5-10 minutes, or until the tofu is heated through and the vegetables are tender. Avoid boiling vigorously as this can break apart the tofu.
4. **Add Leafy Greens**:

1. **Add Greens**: Add the chopped leafy greens to the pot in the last few minutes of cooking. Simmer just until the greens are wilted.
5. **Serve**:
   1. **Ladle into Bowls**: Serve the Yudofu hot, ladling the tofu, vegetables, and broth into individual bowls.
   2. **Dipping Sauces**: Provide dipping sauces such as ponzu or goma-dare for added flavor. Guests can dip their tofu and vegetables into the sauce as they eat.

Tips:

- **Tofu**: Use firm or extra-firm tofu for best results, as it holds its shape better during cooking.
- **Broth**: Adjust the seasoning of the broth to your taste. You can add more soy sauce or mirin if you prefer a stronger flavor.
- **Vegetables**: Feel free to customize the vegetables based on what's in season or what you prefer.

Yudofu is a simple and nourishing dish that highlights the delicate flavor of tofu. It's perfect for a cozy meal and pairs well with a variety of dipping sauces to enhance the taste. Enjoy this comforting Japanese hot pot with family and friends!

Tempura Udon

Ingredients:

- **For the Broth:**
    - 4 cups dashi stock (you can make dashi from scratch or use instant dashi powder)
    - 1/4 cup soy sauce
    - 1/4 cup mirin (sweet rice wine)
    - 2 tablespoons sake (Japanese rice wine)
    - 1 tablespoon sugar (optional, adjust to taste)
- **For the Udon:**
    - 2 servings of udon noodles (fresh or frozen; if using dried, cook according to package instructions)
    - 1-2 green onions, sliced
    - 1/2 cup sliced mushrooms (shiitake, enoki, or button mushrooms)
    - 1/2 cup sliced daikon radish (optional)
    - 1/2 cup bok choy or other leafy greens (optional)
- **For the Tempura:**
    - 1/2 cup all-purpose flour
    - 1/2 cup cornstarch
    - 1/2 teaspoon baking powder
    - 1 cup ice-cold water
    - 1 egg, lightly beaten
    - 1 cup vegetable oil (for frying)
    - Tempura ingredients: shrimp, sweet potato slices, zucchini slices, or any other vegetables of your choice
- **For Garnish (optional):**
    - Shredded nori (seaweed)
    - Sesame seeds
    - Pickled ginger

Instructions:

1. **Prepare the Broth:**
    1. **Combine Ingredients:** In a large pot, combine the dashi stock, soy sauce, mirin, sake, and sugar if using.
    2. **Simmer:** Bring to a gentle simmer over medium heat. Adjust the seasoning to taste.
2. **Cook the Udon Noodles:**
    1. **Boil Noodles:** Cook the udon noodles according to package instructions. Drain and set aside.
3. **Prepare the Tempura:**

1. **Prepare Breading**: In a bowl, combine the flour, cornstarch, and baking powder.
2. **Mix Batter**: In another bowl, whisk together the ice-cold water and beaten egg. Gradually add the dry ingredients to the wet mixture, stirring lightly. The batter should be lumpy.
3. **Heat Oil**: Heat the vegetable oil in a deep pan or fryer to 350°F (175°C).
4. **Coat and Fry**: Dip your tempura ingredients in the batter and fry in the hot oil until golden and crispy, about 2-3 minutes per item. Remove with a slotted spoon and drain on paper towels.

4. **Assemble the Udon**:
    1. **Add Vegetables**: If using mushrooms, daikon, or greens, add them to the simmering broth and cook until tender.
    2. **Add Noodles**: Add the cooked udon noodles to the broth and heat through.
5. **Serve**:
    1. **Ladle into Bowls**: Divide the udon noodles and broth among bowls.
    2. **Top with Tempura**: Place the crispy tempura on top of the noodles.
    3. **Garnish**: Garnish with sliced green onions, shredded nori, sesame seeds, and pickled ginger if desired.

Tips:

- **Batter**: The key to crispy tempura is a cold batter and hot oil. Keep the batter chilled until ready to use and maintain the oil temperature during frying.
- **Tempura Ingredients**: Choose vegetables and seafood that hold up well to frying. Common options include shrimp, sweet potatoes, and zucchini.
- **Broth**: Adjust the broth's seasoning to your taste. You can add a little more soy sauce or mirin if you prefer a stronger flavor.

Tempura Udon is a hearty and satisfying dish that blends the rich, savory flavors of udon broth with the crispy, light texture of tempura. Enjoy this comforting meal with your favorite garnishes and sides!

Miso Ramen

Ingredients:

- **For the Broth**:
    - 4 cups chicken or vegetable broth
    - 1/4 cup white miso paste
    - 2 tablespoons red miso paste (optional, for a richer flavor)
    - 2 tablespoons soy sauce
    - 1 tablespoon mirin (sweet rice wine)
    - 1 tablespoon sake (Japanese rice wine)
    - 1 teaspoon sesame oil
- **For the Ramen**:
    - 2 servings of fresh or dried ramen noodles
    - 1 cup sliced mushrooms (shiitake, enoki, or button mushrooms)
    - 1 cup baby spinach or other leafy greens
    - 1/2 cup sliced bamboo shoots (optional)
    - 1/2 cup corn kernels (optional)
    - 2 green onions, sliced
    - 1 cup cooked and sliced pork belly or chicken (optional)
    - 2 soft-boiled eggs (see instructions below)
- **For Garnish**:
    - Nori (seaweed) strips
    - Sesame seeds
    - Pickled ginger
    - Bean sprouts

Instructions:

1. **Prepare the Broth**:
    1. **Heat Broth**: In a large pot, heat the chicken or vegetable broth over medium heat.
    2. **Mix Miso**: In a small bowl, mix the white miso paste and red miso paste (if using) with a few tablespoons of hot broth to dissolve.
    3. **Combine**: Add the miso mixture to the pot with the broth. Stir well.
    4. **Season**: Add the soy sauce, mirin, sake, and sesame oil to the pot. Simmer for a few minutes, adjusting seasoning to taste.
2. **Cook the Ramen Noodles**:
    1. **Boil Noodles**: Cook the ramen noodles according to package instructions. Drain and set aside.
3. **Prepare Toppings**:
    1. **Cook Vegetables**: In a separate pan, sauté the mushrooms in a little oil until tender. Set aside.

2. **Soft-Boiled Eggs**: To make soft-boiled eggs, gently boil the eggs for about 6-7 minutes, then transfer them to an ice bath to cool. Peel and set aside.
4. **Assemble the Ramen**:
    1. **Add Vegetables and Meat**: Add the cooked mushrooms, bamboo shoots, corn, and spinach to the simmering broth. If using cooked pork or chicken, add that as well. Let simmer until the vegetables are tender and the greens are wilted.
    2. **Add Noodles**: Divide the cooked ramen noodles between bowls.
    3. **Ladle Broth**: Pour the hot miso broth with vegetables and meat over the noodles.
5. **Garnish and Serve**:
    1. **Top**: Halve the soft-boiled eggs and place on top of the ramen. Garnish with sliced green onions, nori strips, sesame seeds, pickled ginger, and bean sprouts if desired.
    2. **Serve**: Serve hot and enjoy!

Tips:

- **Miso**: Adjust the amount of miso paste to taste. White miso is milder and sweeter, while red miso has a stronger flavor. You can use a combination for depth.
- **Noodles**: If using dried ramen noodles, make sure not to overcook them. Fresh noodles are ideal if available.
- **Toppings**: Feel free to customize the toppings based on your preferences. Other options include sliced bamboo shoots, menma (fermented bamboo shoots), and additional vegetables.

Miso Ramen is a comforting and hearty dish that combines the savory richness of miso with the satisfying texture of ramen noodles. Enjoy this delicious bowl of ramen as a warming meal any time of the year!

Soba Noodles with Tempura

Ingredients:

- **For the Soba Noodles:**
    - 8 oz (225 g) soba noodles (buckwheat noodles)
    - 4 cups water (for boiling)
    - 1 tablespoon soy sauce (optional, for added flavor)
- **For the Tempura:**
    - 1/2 cup all-purpose flour
    - 1/2 cup cornstarch
    - 1/2 teaspoon baking powder
    - 1 cup ice-cold water
    - 1 egg, lightly beaten
    - 1 cup vegetable oil (for frying)
    - Tempura ingredients: shrimp, sweet potato slices, zucchini slices, mushrooms, or other vegetables of your choice
- **For the Dipping Sauce (Tsuyu):**
    - 1 cup dashi stock (you can make dashi from scratch or use instant dashi powder)
    - 1/4 cup soy sauce
    - 1/4 cup mirin (sweet rice wine)
    - 1 tablespoon sugar (optional, adjust to taste)
- **For Garnish (optional):**
    - Shredded nori (seaweed)
    - Chopped green onions
    - Sesame seeds
    - Pickled ginger

Instructions:

1. **Cook the Soba Noodles:**
    1. **Boil Noodles**: Bring 4 cups of water to a boil in a large pot. Add the soba noodles and cook according to package instructions (usually 4-6 minutes).
    2. **Drain and Rinse**: Drain the noodles and rinse under cold water to stop the cooking process and remove excess starch. You can also briefly soak them in ice water for extra chill.
    3. **Season (optional)**: Toss the cooked noodles with a little soy sauce if desired. Set aside.
2. **Prepare the Tempura:**
    1. **Prepare Breading**: In a bowl, mix the flour, cornstarch, and baking powder.
    2. **Mix Batter**: In another bowl, whisk together the ice-cold water and beaten egg. Gradually add the dry ingredients to the wet mixture, stirring lightly. The batter should be lumpy.

3. **Heat Oil**: Heat the vegetable oil in a deep pan or fryer to 350°F (175°C).
4. **Coat and Fry**: Dip your tempura ingredients in the batter and fry in the hot oil until golden and crispy, about 2-3 minutes per item. Remove with a slotted spoon and drain on paper towels.

3. **Prepare the Dipping Sauce**:
    1. **Combine Ingredients**: In a saucepan, combine the dashi stock, soy sauce, mirin, and sugar if using.
    2. **Simmer**: Heat over medium heat until the sugar is dissolved and the mixture is warmed. Do not boil. Adjust seasoning to taste.
4. **Assemble the Dish**:
    1. **Serve Noodles**: Place the cooked soba noodles in serving bowls or on individual plates.
    2. **Serve Tempura**: Arrange the tempura on a separate plate or next to the noodles.
    3. **Dipping Sauce**: Serve the dipping sauce in small bowls for dipping the soba noodles and tempura.
5. **Garnish and Enjoy**:
    1. **Garnish**: Garnish with shredded nori, chopped green onions, sesame seeds, and pickled ginger if desired.
    2. **Serve**: Enjoy the soba noodles and tempura with the dipping sauce on the side.

Tips:

- **Batter**: Keep the tempura batter cold and avoid over-mixing to ensure a light, crispy coating.
- **Oil Temperature**: Maintain the oil temperature during frying to ensure the tempura is crispy and not greasy.
- **Noodles**: For a cold soba dish, serve the noodles chilled with the dipping sauce. For a warm version, you can serve the noodles in a hot broth.

Soba Noodles with Tempura offers a wonderful combination of textures and flavors, from the tender soba noodles to the crispy tempura. Enjoy this versatile and satisfying dish either as a main course or a delightful side!

Katsu Curry

Ingredients:

- **For the Katsu (Breaded Cutlet):**
    - 4 boneless pork loin chops or chicken breasts (about 1/2 inch thick)
    - Salt and pepper to taste
    - 1/2 cup all-purpose flour
    - 2 large eggs, beaten
    - 1 cup panko breadcrumbs
    - Vegetable oil (for frying)
- **For the Curry Sauce:**
    - 1 tablespoon vegetable oil
    - 1 onion, finely chopped
    - 2 cloves garlic, minced
    - 1 tablespoon ginger, minced
    - 2 carrots, peeled and sliced
    - 1 potato, peeled and diced
    - 2 tablespoons curry powder (adjust to taste)
    - 2 tablespoons all-purpose flour
    - 3 cups chicken or vegetable broth
    - 1 tablespoon soy sauce
    - 1 tablespoon Worcestershire sauce (optional)
    - 1 tablespoon honey or sugar (optional, for sweetness)
- **For Serving:**
    - Steamed white rice (or Japanese short-grain rice)
    - Sliced green onions (optional)
    - Pickled ginger (optional)

Instructions:

1. **Prepare the Katsu:**
    - **Season the Cutlets**: Season the pork or chicken cutlets with salt and pepper.
    - **Bread the Cutlets**: Dredge each cutlet in flour, then dip into beaten eggs, and coat with panko breadcrumbs.
    - **Heat Oil**: Heat about 1/2 inch of vegetable oil in a large skillet over medium heat.
    - **Fry the Cutlets**: Fry the breaded cutlets in the hot oil until golden brown and cooked through, about 3-4 minutes per side. Remove from the oil and drain on paper towels. Slice the cutlets into strips or leave whole.
2. **Prepare the Curry Sauce:**
    - **Sauté Vegetables**: In a large saucepan, heat the vegetable oil over medium heat. Add the onion and cook until softened, about 5 minutes. Add the garlic and ginger and cook for another minute.

- **Add Carrots and Potatoes**: Add the sliced carrots and diced potatoes. Cook for a few minutes, stirring occasionally.
- **Add Curry Powder and Flour**: Sprinkle the curry powder and flour over the vegetables. Stir well to coat and cook for 1-2 minutes.
- **Add Broth**: Gradually add the chicken or vegetable broth, stirring to prevent lumps. Bring to a simmer.
- **Simmer**: Reduce heat and simmer until the vegetables are tender and the sauce has thickened, about 15-20 minutes.
- **Season**: Stir in the soy sauce, Worcestershire sauce (if using), and honey or sugar (if using). Adjust seasoning to taste.

3. **Serve**:
   - **Prepare Rice**: Serve the Katsu Curry over steamed white rice.
   - **Top with Katsu**: Arrange the sliced or whole cutlets on top of the rice.
   - **Pour Sauce**: Ladle the curry sauce over the cutlets and rice.
4. **Garnish** (optional):
   - Garnish with sliced green onions and pickled ginger if desired.

Tips:

- **Panko Breadcrumbs**: For extra crunch, use Japanese panko breadcrumbs. They are lighter and crispier than regular breadcrumbs.
- **Curry Powder**: Adjust the amount of curry powder to your taste preference. You can also use Japanese curry roux blocks for a more authentic flavor.
- **Serving**: Katsu Curry is traditionally served with steamed rice, but you can also serve it with a side of vegetables or a simple salad.

Katsu Curry is a delicious fusion of crispy cutlets and rich curry sauce, making it a perfect dish for a comforting meal. Enjoy this classic Japanese favorite with family and friends!

Nabe Yaki Udon

Ingredients:

- **For the Broth**:
  - 4 cups dashi stock (can be made from scratch or use instant dashi powder)
  - 1/4 cup soy sauce
  - 1/4 cup mirin (sweet rice wine)
  - 1 tablespoon sake (Japanese rice wine)
  - 1 tablespoon sugar (optional, adjust to taste)
- **For the Nabe Yaki Udon**:
  - 2 servings of udon noodles (fresh or frozen; if using dried, cook according to package instructions)
  - 1/2 cup sliced chicken breast or thigh (or tofu for a vegetarian option)
  - 1/2 cup sliced mushrooms (shiitake, enoki, or button mushrooms)
  - 1/2 cup sliced carrots
  - 1/2 cup bok choy or other leafy greens
  - 1/4 cup sliced green onions
  - 1 egg (optional, for a traditional touch)
  - 1/2 cup fish cakes or other proteins (optional)
  - 1/4 cup cooked shrimp (optional)
- **For Garnish (optional)**:
  - Nori (seaweed) strips
  - Sesame seeds
  - Pickled ginger
  - Shredded daikon radish

Instructions:

1. **Prepare the Broth**:
   - **Combine Ingredients**: In a large pot, combine the dashi stock, soy sauce, mirin, sake, and sugar if using.
   - **Simmer**: Bring to a gentle simmer over medium heat. Taste and adjust seasoning if needed.
2. **Cook the Udon Noodles**:
   - **Boil Noodles**: Cook the udon noodles according to package instructions. Drain and set aside.
3. **Prepare the Nabe Yaki Udon**:
   - **Cook Proteins**: In a separate pan, cook the sliced chicken (or tofu) until fully cooked. If using shrimp, sauté briefly until just cooked. Set aside.
   - **Add Vegetables**: Add the sliced mushrooms, carrots, and fish cakes (if using) to the simmering broth. Cook until vegetables are tender.

        - **Add Noodles and Protein**: Add the cooked udon noodles and the cooked chicken (or tofu) to the broth. Stir to combine and heat through.
        - **Add Greens**: Add the bok choy or other leafy greens and cook until wilted.
        - **Add Egg (optional)**: Crack an egg into the simmering broth, allowing it to poach gently. You can also stir it gently into the broth if you prefer a more mixed texture.
4. **Serve**:
        - **Ladle into Bowls**: Divide the udon noodles, broth, and toppings into individual serving bowls.
        - **Garnish**: Garnish with sliced green onions, nori strips, sesame seeds, pickled ginger, and shredded daikon radish if desired.
5. **Enjoy**:
        - Serve hot and enjoy this warm, comforting dish!

Tips:

- **Broth**: Adjust the seasoning to your taste. If you prefer a richer flavor, you can add a bit more soy sauce or mirin.
- **Vegetables**: Feel free to use other vegetables like snow peas, bell peppers, or bamboo shoots based on your preference.
- **Egg**: The egg adds richness to the dish. If you prefer, you can skip it or use a soft-boiled egg instead.

Nabe Yaki Udon is a versatile and comforting dish, perfect for cold days or whenever you need a hearty, flavorful meal. Enjoy the warm and satisfying combination of udon noodles, savory broth, and fresh ingredients!

Hot Pot with Seafoods

Ingredients:

- **For the Broth:**
    - 4 cups dashi stock (can be made from scratch or use instant dashi powder)
    - 1/4 cup soy sauce
    - 1/4 cup mirin (sweet rice wine)
    - 1 tablespoon sake (Japanese rice wine)
    - 1 tablespoon miso paste (optional, for added depth)
    - 1 tablespoon sugar (optional, adjust to taste)
- **For the Hot Pot:**
    - 1/2 lb (225 g) shrimp, peeled and deveined
    - 1/2 lb (225 g) white fish fillets (such as cod, tilapia, or snapper), cut into bite-sized pieces
    - 1/2 lb (225 g) scallops
    - 1/2 lb (225 g) squid, cleaned and sliced into rings
    - 1 cup sliced mushrooms (shiitake, enoki, or button mushrooms)
    - 1 cup baby bok choy or other leafy greens
    - 1 cup sliced carrots
    - 1/2 cup tofu, cubed
    - 1/2 cup sliced green onions
    - 1 cup bean sprouts (optional)
    - 1 cup udon noodles or soba noodles (optional)
- **For Dipping Sauce (optional):**
    - 1/4 cup soy sauce
    - 1/4 cup rice vinegar
    - 1 tablespoon sesame oil
    - 1 teaspoon sugar
    - 1 teaspoon grated ginger
- **For Garnish (optional):**
    - Chopped fresh cilantro or parsley
    - Sesame seeds
    - Sliced chili peppers (for heat)
    - Pickled ginger

Instructions:

1. **Prepare the Broth:**
    1. **Combine Ingredients:** In a large pot, combine the dashi stock, soy sauce, mirin, sake, and miso paste if using.
    2. **Simmer:** Bring to a gentle simmer over medium heat. Adjust the seasoning with sugar if needed. Keep warm.

2. **Prepare the Ingredients**:
    1. **Prep Seafood**: Clean and cut all seafood into bite-sized pieces. Arrange them on a plate.
    2. **Prep Vegetables**: Slice and prepare all vegetables, tofu, and noodles (if using). Arrange them on separate plates.
3. **Serve the Hot Pot**:
    1. **Heat the Broth**: Bring the pot of broth to a simmer at the table or on the stove.
    2. **Cook Seafood and Vegetables**: Add seafood and vegetables to the simmering broth. Cook until the seafood is opaque and the vegetables are tender, about 2-4 minutes for most items.
    3. **Noodles**: If using noodles, add them to the broth towards the end of cooking and simmer until cooked through.
4. **Prepare Dipping Sauce (Optional)**:
    1. **Combine Ingredients**: Mix the soy sauce, rice vinegar, sesame oil, sugar, and grated ginger in a small bowl.
    2. **Serve**: Use as a dipping sauce for the cooked seafood and vegetables.
5. **Garnish and Serve**:
    1. **Garnish**: Garnish with chopped fresh cilantro or parsley, sesame seeds, sliced chili peppers, and pickled ginger if desired.
    2. **Enjoy**: Serve the hot pot directly from the pot, allowing everyone to enjoy cooking and eating together.

Tips:

- **Seafood**: Choose fresh seafood and adjust the types based on your preferences and availability. You can also use a mix of shellfish and fish.
- **Broth**: You can adjust the flavor of the broth by adding more soy sauce, mirin, or miso paste according to your taste.
- **Vegetables**: Use a variety of seasonal vegetables to add flavor and texture to the hot pot.

Hot Pot with Seafoods is a versatile and enjoyable dish that can be customized to suit your tastes and preferences. It's perfect for sharing with family and friends and makes for a warm and satisfying meal.

Japanese Curry Rice

Ingredients:

- **For the Curry**:
    - 1 tablespoon vegetable oil
    - 1 onion, finely chopped
    - 2 cloves garlic, minced
    - 1 tablespoon ginger, minced
    - 1 pound (450 g) beef (such as chuck or stew meat), cut into bite-sized pieces
    - 2 carrots, peeled and sliced
    - 2 potatoes, peeled and diced
    - 4 cups beef or vegetable broth
    - 1-2 tablespoons soy sauce (adjust to taste)
    - 1-2 tablespoons Worcestershire sauce (optional)
    - 1 tablespoon honey or sugar (optional, for sweetness)
    - 1 package (about 8 oz or 225 g) Japanese curry roux (available in blocks or powder form)
- **For Serving**:
    - Steamed white rice (Japanese short-grain or medium-grain rice works best)
    - Pickles (such as fukujinzuke or rakkyo, optional)

Instructions:

1. **Prepare the Ingredients**:
    1. **Cut Meat and Vegetables**: Cut the beef into bite-sized pieces and peel and chop the vegetables.
2. **Cook the Beef**:
    1. **Sear Meat**: Heat the vegetable oil in a large pot or Dutch oven over medium-high heat. Add the beef pieces and brown on all sides.
    2. **Add Aromatics**: Add the chopped onion, garlic, and ginger. Cook until the onion is softened and translucent.
3. **Add Vegetables**:
    1. **Cook Vegetables**: Add the carrots and potatoes to the pot. Stir to combine with the beef and aromatics.
4. **Add Broth and Simmer**:
    1. **Add Broth**: Pour in the beef or vegetable broth and bring to a boil.
    2. **Simmer**: Reduce heat to low, cover, and simmer for about 30-40 minutes, or until the beef and vegetables are tender.
5. **Add Curry Roux**:
    1. **Incorporate Roux**: Break the curry roux blocks into pieces and add them to the pot. Stir until the roux is completely dissolved and the curry sauce has thickened.

2. **Adjust Seasoning**: Taste the curry and adjust seasoning with soy sauce, Worcestershire sauce, and honey or sugar if needed. Simmer for an additional 5-10 minutes to let the flavors meld.
6. **Serve**:
   1. **Prepare Rice**: Serve the curry over a bed of steamed white rice.
   2. **Garnish**: Optionally, serve with pickles on the side.

Tips:

- **Curry Roux**: Japanese curry roux is available in different levels of spiciness (mild, medium, hot). Choose according to your preference. You can find it in Asian grocery stores or online.
- **Vegetables**: You can add other vegetables like bell peppers or peas based on your taste.
- **Meat Alternatives**: You can use chicken, pork, or even tofu for a vegetarian option.

Japanese Curry Rice is a warm and satisfying dish that's perfect for a family meal. Its rich, flavorful sauce and tender meat and vegetables make it a beloved comfort food in Japan and beyond. Enjoy this classic dish with a side of fluffy rice and pickles for an authentic experience!

Tori Kotsu Ramen

Ingredients:

- **For the Broth**:
    - 4 cups chicken stock (preferably homemade or low-sodium)
    - 2 cups water
    - 1 whole chicken (or chicken bones) for extra richness
    - 1 onion, halved
    - 2 cloves garlic, crushed
    - 1 piece ginger (about 1 inch), sliced
    - 1 leek (white part only), sliced
    - 1-2 dried shiitake mushrooms (optional, for added umami)
    - 2 tablespoons soy sauce
    - 1 tablespoon miso paste (white or red, optional for extra depth)
    - 1 tablespoon sake (Japanese rice wine, optional)
    - Salt, to taste
- **For the Toppings**:
    - 2 servings of ramen noodles (fresh or dried)
    - 2 chicken thighs or breasts, cooked and sliced
    - 1 cup sliced mushrooms (shiitake or enoki)
    - 1 cup baby spinach or bok choy
    - 2 soft-boiled eggs (marinated in soy sauce if desired)
    - 1/4 cup sliced green onions
    - 1 tablespoon sesame oil
    - Nori (seaweed) sheets, cut into strips (optional)
    - Pickled bamboo shoots (menma), for garnish (optional)
    - Bean sprouts (optional)

Instructions:

1. **Prepare the Broth**:
    - **Combine Ingredients**: In a large pot, combine the chicken stock, water, and whole chicken (or chicken bones). Add the onion, garlic, ginger, leek, and dried shiitake mushrooms (if using).
    - **Simmer**: Bring to a boil, then reduce heat to low. Simmer gently for 2-3 hours, skimming off any foam or impurities that rise to the surface.
    - **Strain Broth**: Remove the chicken and vegetables. Strain the broth through a fine-mesh sieve or cheesecloth to ensure it's clear and smooth.
    - **Season**: Stir in the soy sauce, miso paste (if using), and sake. Taste and adjust seasoning with salt if needed. Keep warm.
2. **Prepare the Toppings**:

- **Cook the Chicken**: If using raw chicken thighs or breasts, season and cook them in a pan over medium heat until fully cooked. Slice thinly.
    - **Prepare Vegetables**: Sauté the mushrooms in sesame oil until tender. Set aside.
    - **Soft-Boil Eggs**: To make soft-boiled eggs, bring a pot of water to a boil. Add eggs and cook for 6-7 minutes. Remove and cool in ice water, then peel. For extra flavor, marinate the eggs in a mixture of soy sauce and mirin.
3. **Cook the Noodles**:
    - **Boil Noodles**: Cook the ramen noodles according to package instructions. Drain and rinse under cold water to stop cooking.
4. **Assemble the Ramen**:
    - **Divide Noodles**: Place cooked noodles into bowls.
    - **Add Broth**: Pour hot broth over the noodles.
    - **Add Toppings**: Arrange sliced chicken, sautéed mushrooms, spinach or bok choy, and soft-boiled eggs on top of the noodles.
    - **Garnish**: Sprinkle with sliced green onions, nori strips, pickled bamboo shoots (menma), and bean sprouts if desired. Drizzle with a little extra sesame oil if you like.
5. **Serve**:
    - Serve the ramen hot, and enjoy the rich, flavorful broth with tender noodles and toppings.

Tips:

- **Broth**: For a richer broth, you can add chicken feet or wings along with the whole chicken for a gelatinous texture.
- **Noodles**: Fresh ramen noodles give the best texture, but dried noodles can be used as well.
- **Eggs**: Marinated soft-boiled eggs add extra flavor, but plain soft-boiled eggs are also delicious.

Tori Kotsu Ramen is a satisfying and flavorful ramen dish that highlights the rich, creamy nature of chicken-based broth. It's perfect for a cozy meal and can be customized with your favorite toppings. Enjoy this comforting bowl of ramen!

Tonkotsu Ramen

Ingredients:

- **For the Broth:**
    - 4 pounds (1.8 kg) pork bones (neck bones or femur bones work well)
    - 1 onion, halved
    - 2 cloves garlic, crushed
    - 1 piece ginger (about 2 inches), sliced
    - 1 leek (white part only), sliced
    - 2 dried shiitake mushrooms (optional, for added umami)
    - 12 cups water
    - 1 tablespoon soy sauce
    - 1 tablespoon sake (Japanese rice wine)
    - Salt, to taste
- **For the Toppings:**
    - 2 servings of ramen noodles (fresh or dried)
    - 1/2 pound (225 g) pork belly or shoulder, braised and sliced
    - 2 soft-boiled eggs (marinated in soy sauce if desired)
    - 1 cup sliced mushrooms (shiitake or enoki)
    - 1 cup baby spinach or bok choy
    - 1/4 cup sliced green onions
    - 1 tablespoon sesame oil
    - Nori (seaweed) sheets, cut into strips (optional)
    - Pickled bamboo shoots (menma), for garnish (optional)
    - Bean sprouts (optional)
    - Corn kernels (optional)

Instructions:

1. **Prepare the Broth:**
    - **Blanch Pork Bones:** Place the pork bones in a large pot and cover with water. Bring to a boil, then reduce heat and simmer for 5 minutes. Discard the water and rinse the bones to remove impurities.
    - **Simmer the Broth:** Return the cleaned bones to the pot. Add 12 cups of fresh water, onion, garlic, ginger, leek, and dried shiitake mushrooms (if using). Bring to a boil, then reduce heat to low and simmer, uncovered, for 8-12 hours. The broth should become milky and rich.
    - **Strain the Broth:** After simmering, strain the broth through a fine-mesh sieve or cheesecloth to remove solids. Return the strained broth to the pot. Stir in soy sauce and sake. Adjust seasoning with salt to taste. Keep warm.
2. **Prepare the Toppings:**

- **Braised Pork Belly**: Season the pork belly with salt and pepper, then braise in a pot with some water, soy sauce, sake, and a bit of sugar until tender, about 1.5-2 hours. Slice thinly once cooled.
- **Cook Mushrooms**: Sauté the mushrooms in sesame oil until tender. Set aside.
- **Soft-Boil Eggs**: To make soft-boiled eggs, bring a pot of water to a boil. Add eggs and cook for 6-7 minutes. Remove and cool in ice water, then peel. For extra flavor, marinate the eggs in a mixture of soy sauce and mirin.

3. **Cook the Noodles**:
    - **Boil Noodles**: Cook the ramen noodles according to package instructions. Drain and rinse under cold water to stop cooking.
4. **Assemble the Ramen**:
    - **Divide Noodles**: Place cooked noodles into bowls.
    - **Add Broth**: Pour hot broth over the noodles.
    - **Add Toppings**: Arrange slices of braised pork belly, sautéed mushrooms, spinach or bok choy, and soft-boiled eggs on top of the noodles.
    - **Garnish**: Sprinkle with sliced green onions, nori strips, pickled bamboo shoots (menma), and bean sprouts if desired. Drizzle with a little extra sesame oil if you like.
5. **Serve**:
    - Serve the ramen hot, and enjoy the rich, creamy broth with tender noodles and toppings.

Tips:

- **Broth**: For an even richer broth, consider adding chicken feet or additional pork bones.
- **Noodles**: Fresh ramen noodles provide the best texture, but dried noodles can also be used.
- **Pork Belly**: If braising pork belly, you can use a slow cooker or pressure cooker for convenience.

Tonkotsu Ramen is a deeply satisfying dish with a creamy, savory broth that's perfect for a cozy meal. Enjoy the rich flavors and textures that make this ramen a favorite among many!

Chicken and Mushroom Stew

Ingredients:

- **For the Stew:**
    - 1 tablespoon olive oil
    - 1 pound (450 g) chicken thighs or breasts, cut into bite-sized pieces
    - 1 onion, diced
    - 2 cloves garlic, minced
    - 1 cup carrots, peeled and sliced
    - 1 cup celery, sliced
    - 2 cups mushrooms (such as cremini, button, or shiitake), sliced
    - 1 cup potatoes, diced (optional)
    - 1 cup chicken broth (low-sodium)
    - 1 cup white wine or additional chicken broth
    - 1 tablespoon soy sauce
    - 1 tablespoon Worcestershire sauce (optional)
    - 1 teaspoon dried thyme
    - 1 teaspoon dried rosemary
    - 1 bay leaf
    - Salt and pepper, to taste
    - 1 tablespoon cornstarch mixed with 2 tablespoons water (for thickening, optional)
    - 1/4 cup chopped fresh parsley (for garnish)

Instructions:

1. **Prepare the Ingredients:**
    1. **Cut Chicken**: Cut the chicken into bite-sized pieces and season with salt and pepper.
    2. **Chop Vegetables**: Dice the onion, slice the garlic, carrots, celery, mushrooms, and potatoes (if using).
2. **Cook the Chicken:**
    1. **Heat Oil**: In a large pot or Dutch oven, heat the olive oil over medium-high heat.
    2. **Brown Chicken**: Add the chicken pieces and cook until browned on all sides. Remove from the pot and set aside.
3. **Sauté Aromatics and Vegetables:**
    1. **Cook Onion and Garlic**: In the same pot, add the diced onion and minced garlic. Sauté until the onion is translucent.
    2. **Add Vegetables**: Add the carrots, celery, mushrooms, and potatoes (if using). Cook for about 5-7 minutes, stirring occasionally.
4. **Add Liquids and Seasonings:**
    1. **Deglaze Pot**: Pour in the white wine (or additional chicken broth) and scrape up any browned bits from the bottom of the pot.

2. **Add Broth**: Add the chicken broth, soy sauce, Worcestershire sauce (if using), dried thyme, dried rosemary, and bay leaf.
3. **Return Chicken**: Return the browned chicken pieces to the pot. Stir to combine.
5. **Simmer the Stew**:
    1. **Cook**: Bring the stew to a boil, then reduce heat to low. Cover and let it simmer for 20-30 minutes, or until the chicken is cooked through and the vegetables are tender.
    2. **Thicken Stew**: If you prefer a thicker stew, stir in the cornstarch mixture and cook for an additional 5 minutes until the stew has thickened. Remove the bay leaf before serving.
6. **Garnish and Serve**:
    1. **Garnish**: Sprinkle with chopped fresh parsley.
    2. **Serve**: Serve the stew hot with crusty bread or over rice.

Tips:

- **Mushrooms**: Using a mix of different mushrooms can add depth and variety to the stew.
- **Potatoes**: If you prefer not to use potatoes, you can omit them or replace them with other root vegetables like parsnips.
- **Wine**: The white wine adds flavor, but you can substitute with more chicken broth if you prefer not to use alcohol.

Chicken and Mushroom Stew is a rich, flavorful dish that's perfect for a cozy meal. The combination of tender chicken and savory mushrooms in a delicious broth makes it a comforting classic. Enjoy!

Grilled Daikon

Ingredients:

- 1 large daikon radish
- 1 tablespoon olive oil or vegetable oil
- 1 tablespoon soy sauce
- 1 tablespoon mirin (Japanese sweet rice wine) or honey
- 1 teaspoon sesame oil
- 1 tablespoon rice vinegar
- 1 teaspoon sugar (optional, for added sweetness)
- 1/2 teaspoon sesame seeds (for garnish)
- 2-3 green onions, sliced (for garnish)
- Salt and pepper, to taste

Instructions:

1. **Prepare the Daikon**:
   - **Peel and Slice**: Peel the daikon radish and cut it into thick rounds or wedges, about 1/2 inch (1.5 cm) thick. This helps the daikon cook evenly and develop a nice grill mark.
2. **Preheat the Grill**:
   - **Heat Grill**: Preheat your grill to medium-high heat. If using a stovetop grill pan, preheat it over medium-high heat.
3. **Season the Daikon**:
   - **Mix Marinade**: In a bowl, whisk together the olive oil, soy sauce, mirin (or honey), sesame oil, rice vinegar, and sugar (if using).
   - **Marinate Daikon**: Brush or toss the daikon slices with the marinade, ensuring they are well-coated.
4. **Grill the Daikon**:
   - **Grill**: Place the daikon slices on the grill or grill pan. Cook for about 3-5 minutes per side, or until grill marks appear and the daikon is tender but still crisp. The daikon should have a slightly caramelized exterior.
   - **Check for Doneness**: Test a piece with a fork to ensure it's tender enough. Adjust cooking time as needed depending on the thickness of the slices and the heat of your grill.
5. **Serve**:
   - **Garnish**: Remove the grilled daikon from the grill and transfer to a serving plate.
   - **Add Garnishes**: Sprinkle with sesame seeds and sliced green onions.
6. **Enjoy**:
   - Serve the Grilled Daikon as a side dish, appetizer, or even as a unique addition to salads and bowls.

Tips:

- **Marinating Time**: If you have time, marinate the daikon for 30 minutes to an hour before grilling for even more flavor.
- **Variations**: You can add other seasonings or herbs to the marinade based on your preference, such as garlic or ginger.
- **Grill Marks**: For more pronounced grill marks, avoid moving the daikon slices too much while grilling.

Grilled Daikon is a tasty and healthy option that brings out the natural sweetness of the radish while adding a delightful smoky flavor. It's a versatile dish that pairs well with various Japanese meals or can be enjoyed on its own. Enjoy this unique and flavorful preparation of daikon!

Oyakodon (Chicken and Egg Rice Bowl)

Ingredients:

- **For the Sauce:**
    - 1/2 cup dashi stock (or substitute with chicken or vegetable broth)
    - 1/4 cup soy sauce
    - 1/4 cup mirin (Japanese sweet rice wine)
    - 1 tablespoon sake (Japanese rice wine, optional)
    - 1 tablespoon sugar
- **For the Bowl:**
    - 2 tablespoons vegetable oil
    - 1 onion, thinly sliced
    - 1 cup boneless, skinless chicken thighs or breasts, cut into bite-sized pieces
    - 2 large eggs, lightly beaten
    - 2-3 green onions, sliced (for garnish)
    - 1 tablespoon chopped fresh parsley or shiso leaves (optional, for garnish)
    - 2 cups cooked white rice (steamed)

Instructions:

1. **Prepare the Sauce:**
    - **Mix Sauce Ingredients:** In a small bowl, combine the dashi stock, soy sauce, mirin, sake (if using), and sugar. Stir until the sugar is dissolved. Set aside.
2. **Cook the Chicken and Onions:**
    - **Heat Oil:** In a large skillet or frying pan, heat the vegetable oil over medium heat.
    - **Sauté Onions:** Add the sliced onion and cook until it becomes soft and translucent, about 3-4 minutes.
    - **Cook Chicken:** Add the chicken pieces to the pan and cook until they are no longer pink, about 5-7 minutes, stirring occasionally.
3. **Add Sauce and Simmer:**
    - **Add Sauce:** Pour the prepared sauce over the chicken and onions. Bring to a gentle simmer.
    - **Simmer:** Let it simmer for about 5 minutes, allowing the flavors to meld and the sauce to reduce slightly.
4. **Add Eggs:**
    - **Add Eggs:** Pour the beaten eggs evenly over the chicken and onions. Cover the pan with a lid and cook for 2-3 minutes, or until the eggs are just set but still slightly runny.
5. **Serve:**
    - **Prepare Rice:** Divide the cooked rice between serving bowls.
    - **Top with Chicken and Egg:** Spoon the chicken and egg mixture over the rice.

- **Garnish**: Garnish with sliced green onions and chopped parsley or shiso leaves if desired.
6. **Enjoy**:
    - Serve the Oyakodon hot and enjoy this comforting and flavorful dish.

Tips:

- **Dashi Stock**: If you don't have dashi stock, you can use chicken or vegetable broth as a substitute.
- **Eggs**: For a traditional touch, you can cook the eggs so they remain slightly runny. Adjust the cooking time according to your preference for egg consistency.
- **Rice**: Use short-grain or medium-grain rice for the best texture. Make sure the rice is freshly steamed for the best results.

Oyakodon is a warm, satisfying dish that's easy to make and perfect for a quick weeknight dinner. Its comforting combination of chicken and eggs over rice makes it a favorite in Japanese home cooking. Enjoy this classic bowl of comfort!

Umeboshi and Pork Rice

Ingredients:

- **For the Rice:**
    - 2 cups Japanese short-grain rice
    - 2 1/2 cups water
    - 1/2 teaspoon salt
- **For the Pork and Umeboshi:**
    - 1 tablespoon vegetable oil
    - 1/2 pound (225 g) pork shoulder or pork loin, thinly sliced
    - 1 small onion, thinly sliced
    - 1 tablespoon soy sauce
    - 1 tablespoon mirin (Japanese sweet rice wine)
    - 1 tablespoon sake (optional, can substitute with water)
    - 4-5 umeboshi (pickled plums), pitted and chopped
    - 1 tablespoon sugar (optional, to balance the tartness)
    - 1 teaspoon sesame oil
    - 2-3 green onions, sliced (for garnish)
    - 1 tablespoon sesame seeds (for garnish)

Instructions:

1. **Cook the Rice:**
    - **Rinse Rice**: Rinse the rice under cold water until the water runs clear. This helps remove excess starch.
    - **Cook Rice**: In a rice cooker or pot, combine the rinsed rice, water, and salt. Cook according to your rice cooker's instructions or bring to a boil, then cover and simmer on low heat for 18-20 minutes if using a pot. Let the rice sit covered for 10 minutes after cooking.
2. **Prepare the Pork and Umeboshi:**
    - **Heat Oil**: In a large skillet or pan, heat the vegetable oil over medium-high heat.
    - **Cook Pork**: Add the thinly sliced pork and cook until browned and cooked through, about 5-7 minutes. Remove the pork from the pan and set aside.
    - **Sauté Onion**: In the same pan, add the sliced onion and cook until softened and translucent, about 3-4 minutes.
    - **Add Seasonings**: Return the pork to the pan. Add soy sauce, mirin, sake (if using), and chopped umeboshi. Stir well to combine. If the umeboshi's tartness is too strong, add a tablespoon of sugar to balance the flavors.
    - **Simmer**: Let the mixture cook for another 2-3 minutes, allowing the flavors to meld and the sauce to slightly reduce.
    - **Finish**: Drizzle with sesame oil and stir to combine.
3. **Serve:**

- **Prepare Rice**: Fluff the cooked rice with a fork and divide it between serving bowls.
- **Top with Pork Mixture**: Spoon the pork and umeboshi mixture over the rice.
- **Garnish**: Sprinkle with sliced green onions and sesame seeds.

4. **Enjoy**:
   - Serve hot and enjoy the harmonious blend of flavors and textures.

Tips:

- **Umeboshi**: Umeboshi can be quite sour and salty, so adjust the amount to your taste and consider reducing or omitting the added salt in the rice if you prefer less saltiness.
- **Pork**: Thinly sliced pork is best for quick cooking and blending with the other flavors. You can also use pork belly or ground pork if preferred.
- **Sweetness**: The sugar is optional but can help balance the tartness of the umeboshi, so add according to your taste preference.

Umeboshi and Pork Rice is a delightful dish that combines the bold flavors of pickled plums with savory pork, making it a unique and satisfying meal. Enjoy this tasty Japanese comfort food!

Miso Soup with Clams

Ingredients:

- **For the Soup**:
    - 1 pound (450 g) fresh clams (such as littleneck or Manila), scrubbed and soaked in water with salt for 30 minutes to remove sand
    - 4 cups dashi stock (see note for dashi recipe)
    - 3-4 tablespoons miso paste (white or red miso, depending on preference)
    - 1-2 tablespoons soy sauce (optional, to taste)
    - 1-2 cloves garlic, minced (optional, for extra flavor)
    - 1-2 slices of ginger (optional, for extra flavor)
- **For Garnish**:
    - 2-3 green onions, sliced
    - 1 sheet nori (seaweed), cut into thin strips (optional)
    - 1 tablespoon chopped fresh parsley or cilantro (optional)

Instructions:

1. **Prepare the Clams**:
    - **Soak Clams**: If not already done, soak the clams in a bowl of water with a tablespoon of salt for about 30 minutes to help expel any sand. Rinse and scrub them thoroughly to remove any dirt.
    - **Drain and Rinse**: Drain the clams and rinse them under cold water. Discard any clams that are open and do not close when tapped.
2. **Make the Dashi Stock**:
    - **Prepare Dashi**: You can use homemade or instant dashi stock. To make instant dashi, dissolve dashi powder in water according to the package instructions.
3. **Cook the Clams**:
    - **Heat Dashi**: In a large pot, bring the dashi stock to a simmer over medium heat.
    - **Add Clams**: Add the clams to the pot and cover. Cook for 5-7 minutes or until the clams open. Discard any clams that do not open.
4. **Add Miso Paste**:
    - **Prepare Miso**: In a small bowl, ladle out about 1/2 cup of hot dashi stock from the pot. Whisk in the miso paste until fully dissolved.
    - **Incorporate Miso**: Stir the miso mixture back into the pot with the clams. Be careful not to boil the soup after adding miso, as high heat can alter its flavor.
5. **Adjust Seasoning**:
    - **Taste and Adjust**: Taste the soup and add soy sauce if needed for extra depth of flavor. You can also add minced garlic and ginger at this stage for additional aroma if desired.
6. **Serve**:

- - **Garnish**: Ladle the soup into bowls. Garnish with sliced green onions, nori strips, and chopped parsley or cilantro if desired.
7. **Enjoy**:
   - Serve hot and enjoy the comforting blend of miso and clam flavors.

Tips:

- **Miso**: Use white miso for a milder, sweeter flavor or red miso for a stronger, more robust taste. You can also blend different types of miso to suit your preference.
- **Clams**: Make sure all clams are fresh and well-cleaned. If you cannot find fresh clams, you can use canned clams as a substitute, but adjust the cooking time and seasoning accordingly.
- **Dashi**: Homemade dashi made from kombu (kelp) and bonito flakes provides the best flavor, but instant dashi is a convenient alternative.

Miso Soup with Clams is a delightful and savory soup that highlights the natural sweetness of clams combined with the umami depth of miso. It's a perfect addition to any meal or a warming stand-alone dish. Enjoy!

Salmon and Vegetable Nabe

Ingredients:

- **For the Broth**:
    - 4 cups dashi stock (see note for dashi recipe)
    - 2 tablespoons soy sauce
    - 2 tablespoons mirin (Japanese sweet rice wine)
    - 1 tablespoon sake (optional)
    - 1 tablespoon miso paste (optional, for extra flavor)
- **For the Hot Pot**:
    - 1 pound (450 g) salmon fillets, cut into bite-sized pieces
    - 1 cup mushrooms (shiitake, enoki, or button), sliced
    - 1 cup napa cabbage or bok choy, chopped into bite-sized pieces
    - 1 cup carrots, sliced thinly
    - 1 cup daikon radish, sliced thinly
    - 1 cup tofu, cut into cubes (optional)
    - 1 cup green onions, sliced
    - 1-2 cloves garlic, minced (optional)
    - 1 tablespoon ginger, minced (optional)
- **For Serving**:
    - Cooked white rice or udon noodles (optional)
    - Fresh herbs like shiso or cilantro (optional)
    - Soy sauce or dipping sauce (optional)

Instructions:

1. **Prepare the Broth**:
    - **Heat Dashi**: In a large pot or nabe pot, bring the dashi stock to a simmer over medium heat.
    - **Add Seasonings**: Stir in the soy sauce, mirin, and sake. If using, whisk in the miso paste until fully dissolved.
2. **Prepare the Ingredients**:
    - **Cut Salmon**: Cut the salmon fillets into bite-sized pieces.
    - **Prepare Vegetables**: Slice the mushrooms, chop the cabbage or bok choy, and slice the carrots and daikon radish. Cut the tofu into cubes if using.
3. **Cook the Hot Pot**:
    - **Add Ingredients**: Arrange the salmon, mushrooms, cabbage, carrots, daikon, and tofu (if using) in the simmering broth.
    - **Simmer**: Allow the ingredients to cook until the salmon is opaque and cooked through, and the vegetables are tender, about 5-7 minutes. If using garlic and ginger, add them to the pot for extra flavor.

- **Stir Gently**: Gently stir occasionally to ensure even cooking and to avoid breaking up the salmon pieces.
4. **Serve**:
    - **Prepare Rice or Noodles**: If using rice or noodles, place them in individual bowls.
    - **Ladle Soup**: Ladle the hot pot contents over the rice or noodles.
    - **Garnish**: Garnish with sliced green onions and fresh herbs if desired. Serve with soy sauce or dipping sauce on the side.
5. **Enjoy**:
    - Enjoy the hot pot directly from the communal pot or serve individual portions.

Tips:

- **Dashi**: You can use homemade dashi made from kombu (kelp) and bonito flakes for the best flavor. Instant dashi is also a convenient alternative.
- **Vegetables**: Feel free to customize the vegetables based on what you have on hand or your personal preferences.
- **Broth Flavor**: Adjust the seasoning to taste. If you prefer a richer flavor, you can add a bit more soy sauce or miso.

Salmon and Vegetable Nabe is a delicious and wholesome dish that brings people together around the table. The rich broth and tender ingredients make it a favorite for cozy gatherings. Enjoy this classic Japanese hot pot!

Pork Shogayaki

Ingredients:

- **For the Pork:**
    - 1 pound (450 g) pork loin or shoulder, thinly sliced
    - 2 tablespoons vegetable oil
- **For the Sauce:**
    - 3 tablespoons soy sauce
    - 2 tablespoons mirin (Japanese sweet rice wine)
    - 2 tablespoons sake (Japanese rice wine, optional)
    - 2 tablespoons sugar (adjust to taste)
    - 2-3 tablespoons fresh ginger, grated
    - 1-2 cloves garlic, minced (optional)
- **For Garnish:**
    - 2-3 green onions, sliced
    - 1 tablespoon sesame seeds (optional)
    - Shredded cabbage (optional, for serving)
- **For Serving:**
    - Steamed white rice

Instructions:

1. **Prepare the Pork:**
    - **Slice Pork:** If the pork is not pre-sliced, slice it thinly against the grain. Thin slices cook quickly and absorb the sauce flavors better.
2. **Prepare the Sauce:**
    - **Mix Ingredients:** In a bowl, combine soy sauce, mirin, sake (if using), sugar, grated ginger, and minced garlic (if using). Stir until the sugar is dissolved. Set aside.
3. **Cook the Pork:**
    - **Heat Oil:** In a large skillet or frying pan, heat the vegetable oil over medium-high heat.
    - **Cook Pork:** Add the sliced pork to the pan in a single layer. Cook for about 2-3 minutes on each side, or until the pork is browned and cooked through.
    - **Add Sauce:** Pour the prepared sauce over the pork in the skillet. Stir well to coat the pork evenly.
    - **Simmer:** Continue cooking for another 2-3 minutes, allowing the sauce to thicken and coat the pork. Stir occasionally to ensure the sauce doesn't burn.
4. **Serve:**
    - **Prepare Rice:** Cook and fluff the white rice.
    - **Garnish:** Transfer the pork to serving plates and garnish with sliced green onions and sesame seeds if desired.

- **Accompaniment**: Serve with shredded cabbage on the side, if using.
5. **Enjoy**:
    - Serve the Pork Shogayaki hot over a bowl of steamed rice.

Tips:

- **Ginger**: Freshly grated ginger gives the best flavor. You can adjust the amount of ginger to your taste preference.
- **Pork**: Use pork loin or shoulder for tender results. Thinly sliced pork is ideal for quick cooking and absorbing flavors.
- **Sauce Thickness**: If the sauce is too thin, let it cook a little longer to reduce and thicken. If it's too thick, add a splash of water or broth to reach the desired consistency.

Pork Shogayaki is a flavorful and satisfying dish that's quick to prepare and perfect for a weeknight dinner. The ginger sauce provides a wonderful balance of sweet and savory, making this a favorite in Japanese cuisine. Enjoy this delicious and aromatic dish!

Sukiyaki Udon

Ingredients:

- **For the Sukiyaki:**
    - 1/2 pound (225 g) thinly sliced beef (such as ribeye or sirloin)
    - 1 tablespoon vegetable oil
    - 1 small onion, thinly sliced
    - 1 cup shiitake mushrooms, sliced
    - 1 cup napa cabbage or bok choy, chopped
    - 1 cup carrots, sliced thinly
    - 1 cup tofu, cut into cubes (optional)
    - 2-3 green onions, sliced
    - 2 tablespoons soy sauce
    - 2 tablespoons mirin (Japanese sweet rice wine)
    - 2 tablespoons sake (Japanese rice wine)
    - 2 tablespoons sugar (adjust to taste)
    - 1 cup dashi stock (see note for dashi recipe)
    - 1 tablespoon sesame oil (optional)
- **For the Udon:**
    - 8 ounces (225 g) udon noodles (fresh or frozen)
    - Cooked according to package instructions
- **For Garnish:**
    - 2-3 green onions, sliced
    - 1 tablespoon sesame seeds (optional)
    - Fresh herbs like cilantro or shiso (optional)

Instructions:

1. **Prepare the Ingredients:**
    - **Slice Vegetables:** Thinly slice the onion, shiitake mushrooms, carrots, and chop the cabbage or bok choy.
    - **Prepare Tofu:** Cut tofu into cubes if using.
2. **Cook the Sukiyaki:**
    - **Heat Oil:** In a large skillet or pot, heat the vegetable oil over medium-high heat.
    - **Cook Beef:** Add the sliced beef and cook until browned and cooked through. Remove the beef from the pan and set aside.
    - **Sauté Vegetables:** In the same pan, add the onion and cook until softened, about 3 minutes. Add the shiitake mushrooms, carrots, and cabbage (or bok choy) and cook for another 3-4 minutes until vegetables are tender.
    - **Add Sauce:** Return the beef to the pan. Add soy sauce, mirin, sake, sugar, and dashi stock. Stir to combine and bring to a simmer. Allow to cook for 5 minutes to meld the flavors.

- **Add Tofu**: Gently stir in the tofu cubes if using, and cook for an additional 2-3 minutes. Optionally, drizzle with sesame oil for added flavor.
3. **Cook the Udon**:
    - **Prepare Udon**: Cook udon noodles according to the package instructions. Drain and set aside.
4. **Combine and Serve**:
    - **Add Udon to Sukiyaki**: Add the cooked udon noodles to the sukiyaki mixture in the pan. Stir gently to combine and heat the noodles through.
    - **Garnish**: Serve the Sukiyaki Udon hot, garnished with sliced green onions, sesame seeds, and fresh herbs if desired.
5. **Enjoy**:
    - Serve hot and enjoy the comforting combination of tender beef, vegetables, and udon noodles in a flavorful broth.

Tips:

- **Dashi**: You can use homemade dashi for the best flavor, or instant dashi as a convenient alternative.
- **Beef**: Thinly sliced beef is ideal for quick cooking and blending with the other ingredients. If you prefer a richer taste, you can use a bit more beef or add more sugar.
- **Noodles**: Fresh udon noodles are preferred, but frozen or dried udon can also be used. Be sure to cook them according to the package instructions for the best texture.

Sukiyaki Udon combines the rich flavors of sukiyaki with the chewy texture of udon noodles, making for a hearty and satisfying meal. Enjoy this comforting and delicious dish!

Buta no Kakuni (Braised Pork Belly)

Ingredients:

- **For the Pork:**
    - 1.5 pounds (680 g) pork belly, skin on, cut into 2-inch cubes
    - 1 tablespoon vegetable oil
- **For the Braising Liquid:**
    - 1 cup soy sauce
    - 1 cup mirin (Japanese sweet rice wine)
    - 1 cup sake (Japanese rice wine)
    - 1/2 cup sugar (adjust to taste)
    - 1 cup water
    - 1-2 inches ginger, sliced
    - 2-3 cloves garlic, smashed
    - 2-3 green onions, cut into large pieces
- **For Garnish:**
    - Chopped green onions
    - Sesame seeds (optional)

Instructions:

1. **Prepare the Pork Belly:**
    - **Blanch Pork:** In a large pot, bring water to a boil. Add the pork belly cubes and cook for about 5 minutes. This step helps remove impurities and excess fat. Drain and rinse the pork under cold water. Pat dry with paper towels.
2. **Sear the Pork:**
    - **Heat Oil:** In a large skillet or Dutch oven, heat the vegetable oil over medium-high heat.
    - **Brown Pork:** Add the pork belly cubes and sear on all sides until browned, about 5-7 minutes. Remove the pork from the skillet and set aside.
3. **Prepare the Braising Liquid:**
    - **Combine Ingredients:** In the same skillet or Dutch oven, combine soy sauce, mirin, sake, sugar, water, ginger slices, garlic, and green onions. Stir until the sugar is dissolved.
4. **Braise the Pork:**
    - **Add Pork:** Return the seared pork belly to the skillet with the braising liquid. Bring the mixture to a boil.
    - **Simmer:** Reduce the heat to low, cover, and let it simmer gently for about 2 hours, or until the pork is very tender. Turn the pork occasionally to ensure even cooking.
    - **Reduce Sauce:** After the pork is tender, uncover the pot and continue to simmer for an additional 30 minutes to reduce and thicken the sauce.

5. **Serve**:
   - **Slice and Garnish**: Remove the pork from the sauce and let it cool slightly. Cut the pork into individual pieces, if necessary. Spoon some of the reduced sauce over the pork.
   - **Garnish**: Garnish with chopped green onions and sesame seeds if desired.
6. **Enjoy**:
   - Serve the Buta no Kakuni hot, ideally with steamed white rice and perhaps some pickled vegetables on the side.

Tips:

- **Flavor**: For a more intense flavor, you can marinate the pork in a mixture of soy sauce, mirin, and sake overnight before braising.
- **Fat**: The pork belly will render a lot of fat. You can skim off excess fat from the sauce if you prefer a lighter dish.
- **Adjust Sweetness**: Adjust the amount of sugar to suit your taste. Some like it sweeter, while others prefer a more balanced flavor.

Buta no Kakuni is a rich and indulgent dish that showcases the wonderful flavors of +slow-cooked pork belly. The combination of sweet, salty, and umami flavors creates a deeply satisfying and comforting meal. Enjoy this delicious Japanese classic!

Japanese Beef Stew

Ingredients:

- **For the Stew:**
    - 1.5 pounds (680 g) beef chuck or stew meat, cut into bite-sized pieces
    - 2 tablespoons vegetable oil
    - 1 large onion, sliced
    - 2-3 carrots, peeled and sliced into rounds
    - 2-3 potatoes, peeled and cut into chunks
    - 1 cup mushrooms (shiitake or button), sliced (optional)
    - 2-3 green onions, chopped (for garnish)
- **For the Sauce:**
    - 1/4 cup soy sauce
    - 1/4 cup mirin (Japanese sweet rice wine)
    - 2 tablespoons sake (Japanese rice wine)
    - 2 tablespoons sugar (adjust to taste)
    - 2 cups beef or vegetable broth
    - 1 tablespoon cornstarch mixed with 2 tablespoons water (optional, for thickening)

Instructions:

1. **Prepare the Ingredients:**
    - **Beef:** Cut the beef into bite-sized pieces. Season lightly with salt and pepper.
    - **Vegetables:** Slice the onion, peel and cut the carrots and potatoes, and slice the mushrooms if using.
2. **Sear the Beef:**
    - **Heat Oil:** In a large pot or Dutch oven, heat the vegetable oil over medium-high heat.
    - **Brown Beef:** Add the beef pieces and sear on all sides until browned. This step enhances the flavor of the stew. Remove the beef from the pot and set aside.
3. **Cook the Vegetables:**
    - **Sauté Onions:** In the same pot, add the sliced onions and cook until softened and slightly caramelized, about 5 minutes.
    - **Add Carrots and Potatoes:** Add the carrots and potatoes to the pot, and cook for an additional 3-4 minutes.
4. **Combine Ingredients:**
    - **Return Beef:** Return the seared beef to the pot with the vegetables.
    - **Add Sauce Ingredients:** Pour in the soy sauce, mirin, sake, sugar, and beef or vegetable broth. Stir to combine.
    - **Simmer:** Bring the mixture to a boil, then reduce the heat to low. Cover and simmer for 1-1.5 hours, or until the beef is tender and the vegetables are cooked through. Stir occasionally to ensure even cooking.

5. **Thicken the Sauce** (Optional):
    - If you prefer a thicker sauce, mix the cornstarch with water to make a slurry, and stir it into the stew during the last 10 minutes of cooking. Continue to cook until the sauce has thickened.
6. **Serve**:
    - **Garnish**: Serve the stew hot, garnished with chopped green onions if desired.
    - **Accompaniment**: This stew pairs well with steamed white rice or crusty bread.
7. **Enjoy**:
    - Enjoy the comforting and flavorful stew that highlights the tender beef and rich sauce.

Tips:

- **Beef**: Use a cut of beef that is well-suited for stewing, such as chuck or brisket, for best results.
- **Vegetables**: Feel free to customize the vegetables based on what you have available or your personal preference.
- **Sweetness and Saltiness**: Adjust the amount of sugar and soy sauce to balance the sweetness and saltiness to your taste.

Japanese Beef Stew is a delicious and comforting dish that's perfect for a cozy meal. The combination of tender beef, hearty vegetables, and a savory-sweet sauce makes it a favorite in Japanese home cooking. Enjoy this flavorful stew with family and friends!

Yaki Onigiri (Grilled Rice Balls)

Ingredients:

- **For the Rice Balls**:
    - 2 cups Japanese short-grain rice (or sushi rice)
    - 2 1/2 cups water
    - Salt, to taste
- **For the Glaze**:
    - 2 tablespoons soy sauce
    - 1 tablespoon mirin (Japanese sweet rice wine)
    - 1 tablespoon sake (Japanese rice wine)
    - 1 tablespoon sugar (optional, adjust to taste)
- **For Garnish** (Optional):
    - Toasted nori (seaweed), cut into strips
    - Sesame seeds
    - Pickled plums (umeboshi), for serving

Instructions:

1. **Prepare the Rice**:
    - **Rinse Rice**: Rinse the rice under cold water until the water runs clear. This removes excess starch and helps the rice become sticky.
    - **Cook Rice**: In a rice cooker or a pot, combine the rinsed rice with water. Cook according to the rice cooker's instructions or on the stove until the rice is tender and the water is absorbed. Let it cool slightly.
2. **Shape the Rice Balls**:
    - **Season Rice**: Season the cooked rice with a little salt, mixing gently to distribute the salt evenly.
    - **Shape Rice Balls**: Wet your hands with water to prevent sticking, then take a portion of the rice and shape it into balls or triangles. The traditional size is about 2-3 inches (5-7 cm) in diameter. Press lightly to compact the rice.
3. **Prepare the Glaze**:
    - **Mix Ingredients**: In a small bowl, combine soy sauce, mirin, sake, and sugar (if using). Stir until the sugar is dissolved.
4. **Grill the Rice Balls**:
    - **Preheat Grill**: Preheat a grill or a non-stick skillet over medium heat.
    - **Grill Rice Balls**: Place the rice balls on the grill or in the skillet. Cook for about 2-3 minutes on each side, or until they are crispy and golden brown. If using a skillet, you may need to turn them gently to ensure even grilling.
    - **Apply Glaze**: Brush the glaze onto the rice balls while grilling. Be careful not to burn the glaze; apply it gradually and turn the rice balls to ensure they are evenly coated.

5. **Serve**:
   - **Garnish**: Optionally, garnish with strips of toasted nori or a sprinkle of sesame seeds.
   - **Accompaniments**: Serve with pickled plums (umeboshi) or other favorite side dishes.
6. **Enjoy**:
   - Enjoy the Yaki Onigiri warm, either as a snack or as part of a meal. They are delicious on their own or paired with soups, salads, or grilled meats.

Tips:

- **Rice**: Use Japanese short-grain rice for the best texture. If you can't find Japanese rice, look for other short-grain or sushi rice.
- **Glaze**: The glaze adds a lovely umami flavor and slight sweetness. Adjust the sweetness and saltiness according to your taste.
- **Grilling**: If you don't have access to a grill, a stovetop skillet or grill pan works well. Ensure it is well-oiled to prevent sticking.

Yaki Onigiri are versatile and can be enjoyed in many ways. Their crispy exterior and flavorful glaze make them a great addition to any meal or a tasty snack on their own. Enjoy making and savoring these delightful Japanese grilled rice balls!

Japanese Meatballs (Tsukune)

Ingredients:

- **For the Meatballs**:
  - 1 pound (450 g) ground chicken (preferably with a bit of fat for moisture)
  - 1/2 cup panko breadcrumbs (Japanese breadcrumbs)
  - 1/4 cup grated onion (from about 1 small onion)
  - 1 large egg
  - 2 tablespoons soy sauce
  - 1 tablespoon mirin (Japanese sweet rice wine)
  - 1 tablespoon sake (Japanese rice wine)
  - 1 teaspoon sesame oil
  - 1 teaspoon grated ginger
  - 1 clove garlic, minced
  - Salt and pepper, to taste
- **For the Glaze**:
  - 1/4 cup soy sauce
  - 1/4 cup mirin
  - 2 tablespoons sugar
  - 1 tablespoon sake
- **For Skewering and Garnish** (Optional):
  - Bamboo skewers, soaked in water for 30 minutes to prevent burning
  - Chopped green onions
  - Sesame seeds
  - Shredded nori (seaweed)

Instructions:

1. **Prepare the Meatball Mixture**:
   - **Combine Ingredients**: In a large bowl, combine the ground chicken, panko breadcrumbs, grated onion, egg, soy sauce, mirin, sake, sesame oil, grated ginger, minced garlic, salt, and pepper.
   - **Mix Well**: Use your hands or a spatula to mix the ingredients until well combined. The mixture should be slightly sticky but manageable.
2. **Shape the Meatballs**:
   - **Form Meatballs**: Wet your hands with water to prevent sticking. Take a small portion of the mixture and roll it into a ball about 1.5 inches (4 cm) in diameter. Repeat with the remaining mixture.
   - **Skewer Meatballs** (Optional): If using skewers, gently thread the meatballs onto the skewers, spacing them slightly apart.
3. **Prepare the Glaze**:

- **Combine Ingredients**: In a small saucepan, combine soy sauce, mirin, sugar, and sake.
- **Cook Glaze**: Heat over medium heat until the mixture comes to a simmer and the sugar dissolves. Cook for about 2-3 minutes until slightly thickened. Remove from heat and set aside.

4. **Cook the Meatballs**:
   - **Grill**: Preheat a grill or grill pan over medium heat. Place the skewered meatballs on the grill and cook for about 4-5 minutes on each side, or until they are cooked through and have nice grill marks. Brush with the glaze during the last few minutes of grilling.
   - **Pan-Fry**: Alternatively, heat a non-stick skillet over medium heat. Add a small amount of oil and cook the meatballs, turning occasionally, until they are browned and cooked through, about 10-12 minutes. Brush with glaze during the last few minutes of cooking.
5. **Serve**:
   - **Garnish**: Remove the meatballs from the grill or skillet. If using skewers, you can serve them directly on the skewers or remove the meatballs and place them on a serving plate.
   - **Top with Glaze**: Brush or drizzle extra glaze over the meatballs.
   - **Garnish**: Optionally, garnish with chopped green onions, sesame seeds, and shredded nori.
6. **Enjoy**:
   - Serve the Tsukune warm, either as a stand-alone appetizer or with a side of rice or vegetables.

Tips:

- **Chicken**: Using ground chicken with some fat content will keep the meatballs moist and flavorful. If you prefer, you can use a mix of ground chicken and pork for added richness.
- **Glaze**: Adjust the sweetness and saltiness of the glaze according to your taste. You can also add a bit of grated garlic or ginger for extra flavor.
- **Cooking Method**: If grilling, ensure the grill is well-oiled to prevent sticking. If pan-frying, you may need to add a bit more oil to the pan.

Tsukune are versatile and delicious, with a unique blend of flavors that make them a standout dish. Whether grilled or pan-fried, they offer a taste of Japanese cuisine that's sure to please. Enjoy making and savoring these flavorful meatballs!

Miso-Glazed Eggplant

Ingredients:

- **For the Eggplant:**
    - 2 medium eggplants
    - 2 tablespoons vegetable oil
- **For the Miso Glaze:**
    - 3 tablespoons white miso (shiro miso) or red miso (aka miso)
    - 2 tablespoons mirin (Japanese sweet rice wine)
    - 1 tablespoon sake (Japanese rice wine)
    - 1 tablespoon soy sauce
    - 1 tablespoon sugar (adjust to taste)
    - 1 teaspoon sesame oil (optional, for added flavor)
    - 1 clove garlic, minced (optional)
- **For Garnish** (Optional):
    - Chopped green onions
    - Sesame seeds
    - Toasted nori (seaweed), cut into strips

Instructions:

1. **Prepare the Eggplant:**
    1. **Slice Eggplant:** Cut the eggplants in half lengthwise. You can also cut them into thick slices if preferred.
    2. **Salt Eggplant:** Lightly sprinkle the cut surfaces of the eggplants with salt and let them sit for about 20 minutes. This helps to draw out excess moisture and reduces bitterness. Rinse off the salt and pat the eggplants dry with paper towels.
2. **Prepare the Miso Glaze:**
    1. **Combine Ingredients:** In a small bowl, whisk together the white miso, mirin, sake, soy sauce, sugar, and sesame oil (if using). Mix until the glaze is smooth and well combined.
    2. **Add Garlic:** If using garlic, mix it into the glaze.
3. **Cook the Eggplant:**
    1. **Preheat Oven:** Preheat your oven to 400°F (200°C) or prepare a grill.
    2. **Oil and Arrange:** Brush the cut sides of the eggplants with vegetable oil and place them cut side up on a baking sheet lined with parchment paper or aluminum foil.
    3. **Roast:** Roast the eggplants in the preheated oven for about 20-25 minutes, or until they are tender and starting to brown. If using a grill, cook the eggplants over medium heat until tender.
4. **Apply Miso Glaze:**

1. **Brush Glaze**: Once the eggplants are cooked, remove them from the oven or grill. Brush the miso glaze generously over the cut surfaces of the eggplants.
2. **Broil**: Return the eggplants to the oven and set the oven to broil. Broil for an additional 5 minutes or until the glaze is bubbly and slightly caramelized. Keep a close eye on them to prevent burning.

5. **Serve**:
    1. **Garnish**: Remove the eggplants from the oven and let them cool slightly. Garnish with chopped green onions, sesame seeds, and strips of toasted nori if desired.
    2. **Enjoy**: Serve the Miso-Glazed Eggplant warm as a side dish, appetizer, or main course.

Tips:

- **Eggplant**: Choose eggplants that are firm and free of blemishes. Japanese eggplants or Chinese eggplants work particularly well for this recipe due to their tender texture.
- **Glaze**: Adjust the sweetness and saltiness of the glaze to your taste. You can also experiment with adding a touch of ginger or other seasonings to the glaze.
- **Cooking Method**: If you prefer not to use the broiler, you can also cook the glazed eggplants in the oven at a slightly higher temperature (around 425°F or 220°C) until the glaze caramelizes.

Miso-Glazed Eggplant is a flavorful and visually appealing dish that's easy to prepare. The combination of savory miso and tender eggplant makes it a delightful addition to any meal. Enjoy this Japanese favorite!

Sweet Potato Tempura

Ingredients:

- **For the Tempura**:
    - 2 medium sweet potatoes
    - 1 cup all-purpose flour
    - 1/2 cup cornstarch
    - 1 teaspoon baking powder
    - 1 cup cold sparkling water (or ice-cold water)
    - 1 egg (optional, for a richer batter)
    - Vegetable oil, for frying
- **For Serving** (Optional):
    - Tempura dipping sauce (Tentsuyu), or soy sauce
    - Grated daikon radish
    - Lemon wedges
    - Sea salt

Instructions:

1. **Prepare the Sweet Potatoes**:
    1. **Peel and Slice**: Peel the sweet potatoes and cut them into thin slices or sticks, about 1/4 to 1/2 inch thick. For a more uniform texture, try to keep the pieces similar in size.
    2. **Soak**: Place the sweet potato slices in a bowl of cold water and let them soak for 10-15 minutes to remove excess starch. Drain and pat them dry with paper towels.
2. **Prepare the Tempura Batter**:
    1. **Mix Dry Ingredients**: In a large bowl, combine the flour, cornstarch, and baking powder. Whisk together to ensure they are evenly mixed.
    2. **Add Wet Ingredients**: In a separate bowl, lightly beat the egg (if using), then add the cold sparkling water. Pour the wet ingredients into the dry ingredients and mix gently. The batter should be lumpy and not overmixed; this helps create a light and crispy texture.
3. **Heat the Oil**:
    1. **Preheat Oil**: In a deep pan or heavy-bottomed pot, heat about 2-3 inches of vegetable oil over medium-high heat to 350°F (175°C). Use a thermometer to monitor the temperature.
4. **Fry the Sweet Potatoes**:
    1. **Coat**: Dip the sweet potato slices into the tempura batter, allowing any excess batter to drip off.

2. **Fry**: Carefully slide the battered sweet potatoes into the hot oil. Fry in batches to avoid overcrowding, which can lower the oil temperature. Cook for 2-3 minutes or until the sweet potatoes are golden brown and crispy.
3. **Drain**: Use a slotted spoon to remove the tempura from the oil and place them on a plate lined with paper towels to drain excess oil.

5. **Serve**:
    1. **Garnish**: Serve the Sweet Potato Tempura hot, with a dipping sauce like Tempura dipping sauce (Tentsuyu) or soy sauce. Optionally, you can also serve with grated daikon radish, lemon wedges, or a sprinkle of sea salt.

Tips:

- **Sweet Potatoes**: Choose firm, fresh sweet potatoes for the best results. Japanese sweet potatoes work well, but any variety will do.
- **Batter**: Keep the batter cold and use sparkling water for a lighter, crispier texture. If you prefer, you can omit the egg for a lighter batter.
- **Oil Temperature**: Maintaining the right oil temperature is crucial for crispy tempura. Too hot, and the batter will burn before cooking through; too cool, and it will become greasy.
- **Batter Consistency**: The batter should be lumpy and thick. Over-mixing can lead to a dense coating.

Sweet Potato Tempura offers a sweet and crispy treat that's perfect for any occasion. Whether served as an appetizer or alongside a main dish, this tempura is sure to be a hit. Enjoy making and savoring this Japanese favorite!

Chicken Teriyaki

Ingredients:

- **For the Chicken**:
    - 4 boneless, skinless chicken thighs (or breasts, if preferred)
    - 1 tablespoon vegetable oil (for cooking)
- **For the Teriyaki Sauce**:
    - 1/4 cup soy sauce
    - 1/4 cup mirin (Japanese sweet rice wine)
    - 2 tablespoons sake (Japanese rice wine)
    - 2 tablespoons brown sugar or honey (adjust to taste)
    - 1 clove garlic, minced
    - 1 teaspoon fresh ginger, grated
    - 1 teaspoon cornstarch (optional, for thickening)
- **For Garnish** (Optional):
    - Sesame seeds
    - Chopped green onions
    - Sliced scallions
    - Steamed rice
    - Steamed vegetables (such as broccoli, carrots, or bell peppers)

Instructions:

1. **Prepare the Teriyaki Sauce**:
    1. **Combine Ingredients**: In a small saucepan, combine soy sauce, mirin, sake, brown sugar or honey, minced garlic, and grated ginger.
    2. **Heat and Simmer**: Heat the mixture over medium heat, stirring occasionally until the sugar dissolves and the sauce begins to simmer. If using cornstarch, mix it with a small amount of water to create a slurry and add it to the sauce. Continue to simmer for a few more minutes until the sauce thickens slightly. Remove from heat and let it cool.
2. **Marinate the Chicken**:
    1. **Marinate**: Place the chicken thighs or breasts in a shallow dish or resealable plastic bag. Pour about half of the teriyaki sauce over the chicken, making sure it's well coated. Reserve the remaining sauce for later use. Marinate in the refrigerator for at least 30 minutes, or up to 4 hours for more flavor.
3. **Cook the Chicken**:
    1. **Preheat Pan or Grill**: Heat a grill or a non-stick skillet over medium heat. If using a pan, add vegetable oil to coat the surface.
    2. **Cook Chicken**: Remove the chicken from the marinade and cook on the grill or skillet for 5-7 minutes per side, or until the chicken is cooked through and has an internal temperature of 165°F (75°C). Brush with the reserved teriyaki sauce

during the last few minutes of cooking, turning occasionally to ensure even coating and caramelization.
    3. **Rest**: Once cooked, transfer the chicken to a plate and let it rest for a few minutes before slicing.
4. **Serve**:
    1. **Slice**: Slice the chicken into bite-sized pieces or strips.
    2. **Garnish**: Drizzle with additional teriyaki sauce if desired and garnish with sesame seeds and chopped green onions.
    3. **Accompaniments**: Serve with steamed rice and your choice of steamed or sautéed vegetables.

Tips:

- **Chicken**: Chicken thighs are preferred for their juiciness and flavor, but chicken breasts can also be used if you prefer.
- **Sauce**: Adjust the sweetness and saltiness of the teriyaki sauce to your taste. You can also add a touch of rice vinegar for extra tanginess.
- **Cooking Method**: For a smoky flavor, grilling is ideal. For convenience, pan-frying or baking are also great options.

Chicken Teriyaki is a versatile dish that's both flavorful and easy to prepare. Its sweet and savory glaze pairs wonderfully with rice and vegetables, making it a favorite for family dinners and weeknight meals. Enjoy making and savoring this delicious Japanese classic!

Shrimp Tempura

Ingredients:

- **For the Tempura**:
    - 12 large shrimp, peeled and deveined (tails left on, if desired)
    - 1 cup all-purpose flour
    - 1/2 cup cornstarch
    - 1 teaspoon baking powder
    - 1 cup ice-cold sparkling water (or ice-cold water)
    - 1 large egg (optional, for a richer batter)
    - Vegetable oil, for frying
- **For the Tempura Dipping Sauce** (Tentsuyu):
    - 1/4 cup soy sauce
    - 1/4 cup mirin (Japanese sweet rice wine)
    - 1/4 cup dashi stock (or water if dashi is not available)
    - 1 tablespoon sugar (adjust to taste)
- **For Garnish** (Optional):
    - Grated daikon radish
    - Lemon wedges
    - Chopped green onions
    - Sesame seeds

Instructions:

1. **Prepare the Shrimp**:
    1. **Peel and Devein**: Peel the shrimp, leaving the tails on if desired. Make a few shallow cuts along the length of the underside of the shrimp to prevent them from curling too much during cooking.
    2. **Dry**: Pat the shrimp dry with paper towels.
2. **Prepare the Tempura Batter**:
    1. **Mix Dry Ingredients**: In a large bowl, whisk together the flour, cornstarch, and baking powder.
    2. **Combine Wet Ingredients**: In a separate bowl, lightly beat the egg (if using), then add the ice-cold sparkling water.
    3. **Mix Batter**: Pour the wet ingredients into the dry ingredients and mix gently. The batter should be lumpy and not overmixed; this helps create a light and crispy texture.
3. **Prepare the Tempura Dipping Sauce** (Tentsuyu):
    1. **Combine Ingredients**: In a small saucepan, combine soy sauce, mirin, dashi stock (or water), and sugar.
    2. **Heat and Simmer**: Heat the mixture over medium heat, stirring occasionally until the sugar dissolves. Remove from heat and let it cool.

4. **Heat the Oil**:
   1. **Preheat Oil**: In a deep pan or heavy-bottomed pot, heat about 2-3 inches of vegetable oil over medium-high heat to 350°F (175°C). Use a thermometer to monitor the temperature.
5. **Fry the Shrimp**:
   1. **Coat**: Dip the shrimp into the tempura batter, allowing any excess batter to drip off.
   2. **Fry**: Carefully slide the battered shrimp into the hot oil. Fry in batches to avoid overcrowding, which can lower the oil temperature. Cook for 2-3 minutes, or until the shrimp are golden brown and crispy. Use a slotted spoon to remove the shrimp from the oil and place them on a plate lined with paper towels to drain excess oil.
6. **Serve**:
   1. **Garnish**: Serve the Shrimp Tempura hot, with a dipping sauce such as Tentsuyu. Optionally, garnish with grated daikon radish, lemon wedges, chopped green onions, or sesame seeds.

Tips:

- **Shrimp**: Choose large, firm shrimp for the best results. Ensure they are well-dried before dipping in the batter to prevent excess moisture from causing the batter to become soggy.
- **Batter**: Keep the batter cold and use sparkling water for a lighter, crispier texture. If you prefer, you can omit the egg for a lighter batter.
- **Oil Temperature**: Maintaining the right oil temperature is crucial for crispy tempura. Too hot, and the batter will burn before the shrimp cooks through; too cool, and it will become greasy.
- **Batter Consistency**: The batter should be lumpy and thick. Over-mixing can lead to a dense coating.

Shrimp Tempura offers a delightful crunch and a burst of flavor that's hard to resist. With its crispy exterior and tender interior, it's a dish that's sure to impress. Enjoy making and eating this delicious Japanese classic!

Beef and Vegetable Stir-Fry

Ingredients:

- **For the Stir-Fry:**
    - 1 lb (450 g) beef sirloin or flank steak, thinly sliced against the grain
    - 2 tablespoons vegetable oil (or any neutral oil for stir-frying)
    - 1 red bell pepper, sliced
    - 1 green bell pepper, sliced
    - 1 medium carrot, thinly sliced
    - 1 cup broccoli florets
    - 1 cup snow peas or sugar snap peas
    - 3-4 green onions, sliced
    - 2 cloves garlic, minced
    - 1 teaspoon fresh ginger, grated
- **For the Sauce:**
    - 1/4 cup soy sauce
    - 2 tablespoons oyster sauce
    - 1 tablespoon hoisin sauce
    - 1 tablespoon rice vinegar
    - 1 tablespoon cornstarch (for thickening)
    - 1/2 cup beef broth or water
    - 1 tablespoon brown sugar (optional, adjust to taste)
    - 1 teaspoon sesame oil (optional, for added flavor)
- **For Serving:**
    - Cooked rice (white, brown, or jasmine rice)
    - Sesame seeds (optional)
    - Sliced green onions (optional)

Instructions:

1. **Prepare the Sauce:**
    1. **Mix Ingredients:** In a small bowl, whisk together the soy sauce, oyster sauce, hoisin sauce, rice vinegar, cornstarch, beef broth, and brown sugar (if using). Stir until the cornstarch is fully dissolved.
    2. **Set Aside:** Set the sauce aside.
2. **Prepare the Beef:**
    1. **Slice Beef:** Thinly slice the beef against the grain to ensure tenderness.
    2. **Marinate (Optional):** If you have time, marinate the beef in a little soy sauce and cornstarch for 15-30 minutes for extra flavor and tenderness.
3. **Cook the Vegetables:**
    1. **Heat Oil:** In a large skillet or wok, heat 1 tablespoon of vegetable oil over medium-high heat.

2. **Stir-Fry Vegetables**: Add the garlic and ginger and stir-fry for about 30 seconds until fragrant. Add the bell peppers, carrot, broccoli, and snow peas. Stir-fry for 3-4 minutes, or until the vegetables are crisp-tender. Remove them from the pan and set aside.
4. **Cook the Beef**:
   1. **Heat Oil**: In the same skillet or wok, add the remaining tablespoon of vegetable oil.
   2. **Stir-Fry Beef**: Add the sliced beef and cook for 2-3 minutes, or until browned and cooked through. Make sure not to overcrowd the pan; cook in batches if necessary.
5. **Combine and Finish**:
   1. **Add Vegetables**: Return the cooked vegetables to the skillet with the beef.
   2. **Add Sauce**: Pour the prepared sauce over the beef and vegetables. Stir well to coat everything evenly.
   3. **Cook**: Continue cooking for another 2-3 minutes, or until the sauce has thickened and the vegetables are heated through.
6. **Serve**:
   1. **Prepare Rice**: Serve the Beef and Vegetable Stir-Fry over cooked rice.
   2. **Garnish**: Optionally, garnish with sesame seeds and sliced green onions.

Tips:

- **Beef**: For the best results, use a cut of beef that is tender and well-marbled, such as sirloin or flank steak. Slice the beef thinly and against the grain to ensure it's tender.
- **Vegetables**: Feel free to use any vegetables you like or have on hand. Bell peppers, carrots, broccoli, and snow peas are classic choices, but mushrooms, bok choy, and snap peas are also great options.
- **Cooking**: Stir-frying is a quick process, so have all your ingredients prepped and ready before you start cooking. This ensures a smooth cooking process and prevents overcooking.

Beef and Vegetable Stir-Fry is a delicious and versatile dish that pairs well with rice and can be easily adapted to suit your tastes and available ingredients. Enjoy making and savoring this tasty and wholesome meal!

Japanese-Style Lasagna

Ingredients:

- **For the Meat Sauce:**
    - 1 lb (450 g) ground beef or pork (or a combination)
    - 1 medium onion, finely chopped
    - 2 cloves garlic, minced
    - 1 carrot, finely diced
    - 1 bell pepper, finely diced (optional)
    - 1/4 cup soy sauce
    - 2 tablespoons miso paste (white or red)
    - 1 tablespoon sake (optional)
    - 1 tablespoon sugar
    - 1 can (14 oz/400 g) diced tomatoes
    - 1/2 cup water or beef broth
    - 1 tablespoon vegetable oil
    - Salt and pepper to taste
- **For the Cheese Sauce:**
    - 2 tablespoons butter
    - 2 tablespoons all-purpose flour
    - 1 1/2 cups milk
    - 1 cup shredded mozzarella cheese
    - 1/2 cup grated Parmesan cheese
    - 1 tablespoon soy sauce
    - 1 tablespoon mirin (optional)
    - Salt and pepper to taste
- **For Assembly:**
    - 8-10 lasagna noodles, cooked according to package instructions
    - 1 cup shredded mozzarella cheese
    - 1/2 cup grated Parmesan cheese
    - 2 green onions, sliced (for garnish, optional)

Instructions:

1. **Prepare the Meat Sauce:**
    1. **Cook Meat:** Heat vegetable oil in a large skillet or saucepan over medium heat. Add the chopped onion, garlic, and carrot (and bell pepper if using). Cook until the vegetables are softened, about 5 minutes.
    2. **Add Meat:** Add the ground beef or pork and cook until browned, breaking it up with a spoon.
    3. **Add Flavorings:** Stir in the soy sauce, miso paste, sake (if using), and sugar. Cook for another 2 minutes.

4. **Add Tomatoes**: Add the diced tomatoes and water (or beef broth). Bring to a simmer and cook for 15-20 minutes, until the sauce thickens and the flavors meld. Season with salt and pepper to taste.
2. **Prepare the Cheese Sauce**:
    1. **Make Roux**: In a saucepan, melt the butter over medium heat. Stir in the flour and cook for 1-2 minutes, until it forms a smooth paste.
    2. **Add Milk**: Gradually whisk in the milk and cook, stirring constantly, until the mixture thickens and comes to a simmer.
    3. **Add Cheese**: Stir in the shredded mozzarella cheese and grated Parmesan cheese until melted and smooth.
    4. **Season**: Add soy sauce and mirin (if using), and season with salt and pepper to taste.
3. **Assemble the Lasagna**:
    1. **Preheat Oven**: Preheat your oven to 375°F (190°C).
    2. **Layer**: Spread a thin layer of meat sauce on the bottom of a baking dish. Place a layer of cooked lasagna noodles on top. Spread some cheese sauce over the noodles, then add a layer of meat sauce. Repeat the layers, ending with a layer of cheese sauce on top.
    3. **Top**: Sprinkle the top with shredded mozzarella cheese and grated Parmesan cheese.
4. **Bake**:
    1. **Cook**: Bake in the preheated oven for 25-30 minutes, or until the top is golden brown and bubbly. Let it cool for a few minutes before slicing.
5. **Garnish and Serve**:
    1. **Garnish**: Garnish with sliced green onions if desired.
    2. **Serve**: Serve hot, and enjoy this unique fusion of Japanese and Italian flavors!

Tips:

- **Noodles**: Use traditional lasagna noodles, or you can opt for gluten-free noodles if you prefer.
- **Vegetables**: Feel free to add other vegetables to the meat sauce, such as mushrooms or spinach, for added nutrition and flavor.
- **Cheese**: You can adjust the types and amounts of cheese based on your preference. Adding a bit of cream cheese to the cheese sauce can make it richer and creamier.

Japanese-Style Lasagna combines familiar lasagna elements with Japanese seasonings and ingredients, creating a deliciously unique dish that's sure to impress. Enjoy this comforting meal with a side salad or some steamed vegetables for a complete dinner!

Japanese Potatoes and Beef

Ingredients:

- **For the Dish:**
    - 1 lb (450 g) beef sirloin or chuck, cut into bite-sized cubes
    - 4 medium potatoes, peeled and cut into bite-sized chunks
    - 1 medium onion, sliced
    - 1 carrot, sliced (optional)
    - 1 tablespoon vegetable oil
    - 1 cup dashi stock (or water with dashi powder)
    - 1/4 cup soy sauce
    - 2 tablespoons mirin
    - 2 tablespoons sugar
    - 1 tablespoon sake (optional)
    - 2 green onions, chopped (for garnish, optional)
    - Sesame seeds (for garnish, optional)

Instructions:

1. **Prepare the Ingredients:**
    1. **Cut Beef:** Cut the beef into bite-sized cubes.
    2. **Prepare Vegetables:** Peel and cut the potatoes into chunks. Slice the onion and carrot (if using).
2. **Cook the Beef:**
    1. **Heat Oil:** In a large pot or Dutch oven, heat the vegetable oil over medium-high heat.
    2. **Brown Beef:** Add the beef cubes and cook until browned on all sides. This should take about 5-7 minutes.
3. **Add Vegetables:**
    1. **Add Onion:** Add the sliced onion to the pot and cook until softened, about 3-4 minutes.
    2. **Add Carrot and Potatoes:** Add the sliced carrot (if using) and potato chunks to the pot.
4. **Prepare the Sauce:**
    1. **Combine Ingredients:** In a bowl, combine the dashi stock, soy sauce, mirin, sugar, and sake (if using). Stir until the sugar is dissolved.
5. **Simmer:**
    1. **Add Sauce:** Pour the sauce mixture over the beef and vegetables in the pot.
    2. **Simmer:** Bring to a boil, then reduce the heat to low. Cover and simmer for about 20-25 minutes, or until the potatoes and beef are tender and the sauce has thickened slightly.
6. **Finish and Serve:**

1. **Adjust Seasoning**: Taste the sauce and adjust seasoning with additional soy sauce or sugar if needed.
2. **Garnish**: Garnish with chopped green onions and sesame seeds, if desired.
3. **Serve**: Serve hot over steamed rice or enjoy on its own.

Tips:

- **Beef**: For a tender result, use cuts of beef that are well-suited for simmering, like sirloin or chuck.
- **Dashi**: Dashi is a key ingredient in Japanese cooking and adds a depth of umami flavor. You can use instant dashi powder mixed with water if you don't have ready-made dashi stock.
- **Potatoes**: Choose waxy potatoes that hold their shape well during cooking, such as Yukon Gold or red potatoes.

Japanese Potatoes and Beef is a comforting and hearty dish that's perfect for cold days or when you need a satisfying meal. The rich, savory sauce and tender beef combined with soft potatoes make it a dish that's sure to please. Enjoy preparing and eating this flavorful Japanese classic!

Pork and Daikon Radish Stew

Ingredients:

- **For the Stew:**
    - 1 lb (450 g) pork belly or pork shoulder, cut into bite-sized cubes
    - 1 large daikon radish, peeled and cut into bite-sized chunks
    - 1 medium carrot, sliced (optional)
    - 1 onion, sliced
    - 2 cloves garlic, minced
    - 1 tablespoon ginger, minced
    - 1 tablespoon vegetable oil
    - 4 cups dashi stock (or water with dashi powder)
    - 1/4 cup soy sauce
    - 2 tablespoons mirin
    - 1 tablespoon sugar
    - 2 tablespoons sake (optional)
    - 2 green onions, sliced (for garnish, optional)
    - Sesame seeds (for garnish, optional)

Instructions:

1. **Prepare the Ingredients:**
    1. **Cut Pork:** Cut the pork into bite-sized cubes.
    2. **Prepare Vegetables:** Peel and cut the daikon radish into chunks. Slice the carrot (if using) and onion.
2. **Cook the Pork:**
    1. **Heat Oil:** In a large pot or Dutch oven, heat the vegetable oil over medium-high heat.
    2. **Brown Pork:** Add the pork cubes and cook until browned on all sides. This should take about 5-7 minutes.
3. **Add Vegetables:**
    1. **Add Onion and Aromatics:** Add the sliced onion, garlic, and ginger to the pot. Cook until the onion is softened and translucent, about 3-4 minutes.
    2. **Add Daikon and Carrot:** Add the daikon radish and carrot to the pot.
4. **Prepare the Broth:**
    1. **Combine Ingredients:** In a bowl, combine the dashi stock, soy sauce, mirin, sugar, and sake (if using). Stir until the sugar is dissolved.
5. **Simmer:**
    1. **Add Broth:** Pour the broth mixture over the pork and vegetables in the pot.
    2. **Simmer:** Bring to a boil, then reduce the heat to low. Cover and simmer for about 30-40 minutes, or until the pork and daikon are tender and the flavors are well combined. Stir occasionally and skim off any foam or fat that rises to the surface.

6. **Finish and Serve**:
    1. **Adjust Seasoning**: Taste the stew and adjust seasoning with additional soy sauce or sugar if needed.
    2. **Garnish**: Garnish with sliced green onions and sesame seeds, if desired.
    3. **Serve**: Serve hot, either on its own or over steamed rice.

Tips:

- **Pork**: Pork belly provides a rich flavor, but pork shoulder or other cuts can be used as well. If using a leaner cut, you might want to add a bit more oil or adjust the cooking time to ensure tenderness.
- **Daikon**: Daikon radish is a key ingredient that absorbs the flavors of the broth. If you can't find daikon, you can substitute with other types of radish or even potatoes.
- **Dashi**: Dashi adds a depth of umami flavor to the stew. If you don't have dashi, you can use a good-quality chicken or vegetable broth as a substitute.

Pork and Daikon Radish Stew is a comforting and flavorful dish that showcases the best of Japanese home cooking. The combination of tender pork and daikon in a savory broth makes it a satisfying and warming meal. Enjoy preparing and savoring this traditional Japanese stew!

Simmered Kabocha Squash

Ingredients:

- 1 medium kabocha squash (about 2-3 lbs/900-1300 g)
- 2 tablespoons vegetable oil
- 1/4 cup soy sauce
- 1/4 cup mirin
- 2 tablespoons sugar
- 1 cup dashi stock (or water with dashi powder)
- 1 tablespoon sake (optional)
- 1 tablespoon sesame seeds (for garnish, optional)
- 2 green onions, sliced (for garnish, optional)

Instructions:

1. **Prepare the Kabocha Squash**:
    1. **Cut the Squash**: Slice the kabocha squash in half, remove the seeds, and cut it into bite-sized chunks. You can leave the skin on, as it becomes tender during cooking and adds texture.
2. **Cook the Squash**:
    1. **Heat Oil**: In a large skillet or saucepan, heat the vegetable oil over medium heat.
    2. **Sauté Squash**: Add the kabocha squash chunks to the skillet and cook for 2-3 minutes, turning occasionally, until they start to lightly brown.
3. **Prepare the Sauce**:
    1. **Combine Ingredients**: In a bowl, mix together the soy sauce, mirin, sugar, dashi stock, and sake (if using). Stir until the sugar is dissolved.
4. **Simmer**:
    1. **Add Sauce**: Pour the sauce mixture over the squash in the skillet.
    2. **Simmer**: Bring to a boil, then reduce the heat to low. Cover and simmer for about 15-20 minutes, or until the squash is tender and the sauce has thickened slightly. Check occasionally and add a bit more water if the sauce reduces too quickly.
5. **Finish and Serve**:
    1. **Adjust Seasoning**: Taste the sauce and adjust seasoning with additional soy sauce or sugar if needed.
    2. **Garnish**: Garnish with sesame seeds and sliced green onions, if desired.
    3. **Serve**: Serve warm or at room temperature as a side dish.

Tips:

- **Kabocha Squash**: Kabocha squash is a Japanese pumpkin with a sweet flavor and creamy texture. If you can't find kabocha, you can use other types of squash like butternut or acorn squash as substitutes.

- **Dashi**: Dashi stock adds a depth of umami flavor. If you don't have dashi, you can use a good-quality vegetable or chicken broth.
- **Consistency**: If you prefer a thicker sauce, you can simmer the dish uncovered for the last few minutes to reduce the sauce further.

Simmered Kabocha Squash is a delightful and comforting dish that's easy to make and brings out the best of this autumnal vegetable. Its sweet and savory flavor makes it a versatile side that complements a wide range of Japanese meals. Enjoy preparing and savoring this delicious dish!

Tofu and Vegetable Stir-Fry

Ingredients:

- **For the Stir-Fry**:
    - 14 oz (400 g) firm tofu, drained and cubed
    - 1 tablespoon vegetable oil (or sesame oil)
    - 1 red bell pepper, sliced
    - 1 cup broccoli florets
    - 1 medium carrot, sliced
    - 1 cup snap peas or snow peas
    - 1 small onion, sliced
    - 2 cloves garlic, minced
    - 1 tablespoon fresh ginger, minced
    - 2-3 green onions, sliced (for garnish, optional)
    - Sesame seeds (for garnish, optional)
- **For the Stir-Fry Sauce**:
    - 1/4 cup soy sauce
    - 2 tablespoons hoisin sauce (or oyster sauce for a non-vegetarian option)
    - 1 tablespoon rice vinegar (or apple cider vinegar)
    - 1 tablespoon sesame oil
    - 1 tablespoon cornstarch mixed with 2 tablespoons water (for thickening)
    - 1 teaspoon sugar or honey (optional, for extra sweetness)
    - 1/2 teaspoon chili flakes (optional, for heat)

Instructions:

1. **Prepare the Tofu**:
    1. **Drain Tofu**: Press the tofu to remove excess moisture. You can do this by wrapping the tofu in a clean kitchen towel and placing a heavy object on top for 10-15 minutes.
    2. **Cube Tofu**: Cut the tofu into bite-sized cubes.
2. **Prepare the Vegetables**:
    1. **Cut Vegetables**: Slice the bell pepper, onion, and carrot. Cut the broccoli into florets and prepare the snap peas or snow peas.
3. **Cook the Tofu**:
    1. **Heat Oil**: In a large skillet or wok, heat the vegetable oil over medium-high heat.
    2. **Cook Tofu**: Add the tofu cubes to the skillet and cook, turning occasionally, until golden brown and crispy on all sides, about 5-7 minutes. Remove tofu from the skillet and set aside.
4. **Stir-Fry the Vegetables**:
    1. **Add Aromatics**: In the same skillet, add a bit more oil if needed. Add the sliced onion, garlic, and ginger. Cook for 1-2 minutes until fragrant.

2. **Add Vegetables**: Add the bell pepper, broccoli, carrot, and snap peas. Stir-fry for about 5 minutes, or until the vegetables are tender-crisp.
5. **Prepare the Sauce**:
    1. **Combine Sauce Ingredients**: In a bowl, whisk together the soy sauce, hoisin sauce, rice vinegar, sesame oil, cornstarch-water mixture, sugar (if using), and chili flakes (if using).
6. **Combine Everything**:
    1. **Add Tofu**: Return the cooked tofu to the skillet with the vegetables.
    2. **Add Sauce**: Pour the sauce over the tofu and vegetables. Stir well to coat everything evenly. Cook for another 2-3 minutes until the sauce has thickened and everything is heated through.
7. **Finish and Serve**:
    1. **Garnish**: Garnish with sliced green onions and sesame seeds, if desired.
    2. **Serve**: Serve hot over steamed rice or noodles.

Tips:

- **Tofu**: For extra flavor, marinate the tofu in a bit of soy sauce and sesame oil before cooking.
- **Vegetables**: Feel free to use any vegetables you have on hand or prefer. Bell peppers, mushrooms, baby corn, and bok choy are great additions.
- **Sauce Thickness**: Adjust the amount of cornstarch or water to achieve your desired sauce consistency.

Tofu and Vegetable Stir-Fry is a versatile dish that's packed with flavor and nutrition. It's quick to prepare, making it perfect for busy weeknights or a healthy lunch. Enjoy this colorful and delicious stir-fry!

Salmon and Cabbage Stew

Ingredients:

- **For the Stew:**
    - 1 lb (450 g) salmon fillets, skinless and boneless, cut into bite-sized pieces
    - 1 small head of cabbage, chopped into bite-sized pieces
    - 1 medium onion, sliced
    - 2 cloves garlic, minced
    - 1 medium carrot, sliced
    - 2 tablespoons vegetable oil (or sesame oil)
    - 4 cups fish stock (or water with fish bouillon) or chicken stock
    - 2 tablespoons soy sauce
    - 1 tablespoon miso paste (white or yellow)
    - 1 tablespoon mirin (optional)
    - 1 teaspoon grated ginger
    - 1 tablespoon sake (optional)
    - 2 green onions, sliced (for garnish, optional)
    - Fresh herbs for garnish (such as parsley or cilantro, optional)

Instructions:

1. **Prepare the Ingredients:**
    1. **Cut Salmon**: Cut the salmon into bite-sized pieces.
    2. **Chop Vegetables**: Chop the cabbage into bite-sized pieces, slice the onion, and slice the carrot. Mince the garlic and grate the ginger.
2. **Cook the Aromatics:**
    1. **Heat Oil**: In a large pot or Dutch oven, heat the vegetable oil over medium heat.
    2. **Sauté Aromatics**: Add the sliced onion, garlic, and grated ginger. Cook for about 3-4 minutes, or until the onion is softened and fragrant.
3. **Add Vegetables:**
    1. **Add Carrot and Cabbage**: Add the sliced carrot and chopped cabbage to the pot. Stir and cook for an additional 5 minutes, until the cabbage starts to wilt.
4. **Prepare the Broth:**
    1. **Combine Broth Ingredients**: In a bowl, mix the fish stock (or chicken stock), soy sauce, miso paste, and mirin (if using). Stir until the miso paste is dissolved.
5. **Simmer the Stew:**
    1. **Add Broth**: Pour the broth mixture into the pot with the vegetables. Stir to combine.
    2. **Simmer**: Bring to a boil, then reduce the heat to low. Cover and simmer for about 15 minutes, or until the cabbage and carrots are tender.
6. **Add Salmon:**

1. **Add Salmon**: Gently add the salmon pieces to the pot. Simmer for an additional 5-7 minutes, or until the salmon is cooked through and flakes easily.
7. **Finish and Serve**:
    1. **Adjust Seasoning**: Taste the stew and adjust seasoning with additional soy sauce or miso paste if needed.
    2. **Garnish**: Garnish with sliced green onions and fresh herbs, if desired.
    3. **Serve**: Serve hot, either on its own or with steamed rice.

Tips:

- **Salmon**: Use fresh or frozen salmon fillets. If using frozen, make sure to thaw them properly before cooking.
- **Miso**: Miso paste adds depth of flavor. If you prefer a stronger miso taste, you can use red miso, but white or yellow miso is more common for a lighter flavor.
- **Vegetables**: Feel free to add other vegetables you like, such as mushrooms or bell peppers.

Salmon and Cabbage Stew is a hearty and nourishing dish that brings together the delicate flavors of salmon with the satisfying texture of cabbage. It's a great choice for a warming and wholesome meal. Enjoy making and savoring this comforting stew!

Nabeyaki Ramen

Ingredients:

- **For the Ramen:**
    - 2 servings of fresh or dried ramen noodles
    - 1 tablespoon vegetable oil (or sesame oil)
    - 1 small onion, sliced
    - 2 cloves garlic, minced
    - 1-inch piece of ginger, minced
    - 1 cup sliced mushrooms (shiitake, button, or any preferred variety)
    - 1 small carrot, thinly sliced
    - 1 cup bok choy or spinach
    - 1 cup sliced cooked chicken, pork, or seafood (optional)
    - 4 cups chicken or vegetable broth
    - 1 tablespoon soy sauce
    - 1 tablespoon miso paste (optional, for added depth of flavor)
    - 1 tablespoon mirin (optional, for a touch of sweetness)
    - 1 teaspoon sesame oil (for finishing)
    - 2 green onions, sliced (for garnish)
    - Nori (seaweed) strips (for garnish)
    - 1 egg (per serving, optional, for soft-boiled or poached)

Instructions:

1. **Prepare the Ingredients:**
    - **Cook the Noodles:** Cook the ramen noodles according to the package instructions. Drain and set aside.
    - **Prepare Vegetables:** Slice the onion, mince the garlic and ginger, and slice the mushrooms and carrot. Prepare any additional proteins like chicken, pork, or seafood if using.
2. **Cook the Aromatics:**
    - **Heat Oil:** In a large pot or Dutch oven, heat the vegetable oil over medium heat.
    - **Sauté Aromatics:** Add the sliced onion, garlic, and ginger. Cook for about 3-4 minutes, until the onion is softened and fragrant.
3. **Add Vegetables:**
    - **Add Mushrooms and Carrot:** Add the sliced mushrooms and carrot to the pot. Cook for about 5 minutes, stirring occasionally, until the vegetables begin to soften.
4. **Prepare the Broth:**
    - **Add Broth:** Pour the chicken or vegetable broth into the pot with the vegetables.
    - **Season:** Stir in the soy sauce, miso paste (if using), and mirin (if using). Bring the broth to a boil, then reduce the heat and let it simmer for about 10 minutes.

5. **Add Protein and Greens**:
   - **Add Protein**: If using pre-cooked chicken, pork, or seafood, add it to the pot to heat through.
   - **Add Greens**: Add the bok choy or spinach to the pot and cook for another 2-3 minutes, until the greens are wilted.
6. **Assemble the Ramen**:
   - **Add Noodles**: Divide the cooked ramen noodles between serving bowls.
   - **Pour Broth**: Ladle the hot broth and vegetables over the noodles.
   - **Garnish**: Top each bowl with sliced green onions, nori strips, and a drizzle of sesame oil.
7. **Add Egg (Optional)**:
   - **Prepare Egg**: If adding an egg, you can either soft-boil or poach it. To soft-boil, cook the egg in boiling water for 6-7 minutes, then peel and halve. To poach, add the egg directly to the simmering broth and cook until the white is set but the yolk is still runny.
8. **Serve**:
   - Serve the Nabeyaki Ramen hot, allowing everyone to mix the ingredients together as they eat.

Tips:

- **Broth**: For a richer broth, you can use homemade chicken or vegetable stock, or add a splash of sake or white wine for extra depth.
- **Noodles**: Fresh ramen noodles work best, but you can also use dried noodles if needed. Adjust the cooking time according to the package instructions.
- **Vegetables**: Feel free to customize the vegetables based on what's in season or your preferences.

Nabeyaki Ramen combines the heartiness of a ramen bowl with the warmth and comfort of a hot pot. It's a versatile dish that can be adapted to suit various tastes and is perfect for a satisfying meal. Enjoy making and savoring this delicious and comforting ramen stew!

Braised Chicken with Shiitake Mushrooms

Ingredients:

- **For the Braise:**
    - 4 bone-in, skinless chicken thighs (or 4 chicken breasts)
    - 1 cup dried shiitake mushrooms (or 1 cup fresh shiitake mushrooms, sliced)
    - 1 tablespoon vegetable oil (or sesame oil)
    - 1 medium onion, sliced
    - 2 cloves garlic, minced
    - 1-inch piece of ginger, minced
    - 1/2 cup soy sauce
    - 1/4 cup mirin (or dry white wine)
    - 1/4 cup sake (optional) or additional water
    - 2 tablespoons sugar (or honey)
    - 1 cup chicken broth
    - 2 green onions, sliced (for garnish, optional)
    - 1 tablespoon sesame seeds (for garnish, optional)

Instructions:

1. **Prepare the Mushrooms:**
    1. **Rehydrate Dried Mushrooms:** If using dried shiitake mushrooms, soak them in warm water for about 20-30 minutes until they are soft. Drain and slice. If using fresh mushrooms, simply slice them.
2. **Prepare the Chicken:**
    1. **Season Chicken:** Season the chicken thighs with salt and pepper.
3. **Brown the Chicken:**
    1. **Heat Oil:** In a large, heavy-bottomed pot or Dutch oven, heat the vegetable oil over medium-high heat.
    2. **Brown Chicken:** Add the chicken thighs to the pot and brown on both sides for about 3-4 minutes per side. Remove the chicken from the pot and set aside.
4. **Cook Aromatics:**
    1. **Sauté Aromatics:** In the same pot, add a bit more oil if needed. Sauté the sliced onion, garlic, and ginger for about 3-4 minutes until the onion is softened and fragrant.
5. **Add Mushrooms and Sauce Ingredients:**
    1. **Add Mushrooms:** Add the shiitake mushrooms to the pot and cook for an additional 2-3 minutes.
    2. **Add Sauce:** Pour in the soy sauce, mirin, sake (if using), sugar, and chicken broth. Stir to combine.
6. **Braise the Chicken:**

1. **Return Chicken**: Return the browned chicken thighs to the pot, making sure they are submerged in the sauce.
   2. **Simmer**: Bring to a boil, then reduce the heat to low. Cover and simmer for about 30-40 minutes, or until the chicken is tender and cooked through.
7. **Finish and Serve**:
   1. **Adjust Seasoning**: Taste the sauce and adjust the seasoning with additional soy sauce or sugar if needed.
   2. **Garnish**: Garnish with sliced green onions and sesame seeds, if desired.
   3. **Serve**: Serve the braised chicken with shiitake mushrooms over steamed rice or noodles.

Tips:

- **Chicken**: Bone-in, skinless chicken thighs are ideal for braising as they stay tender and flavorful. You can use chicken breasts, but they may be less tender.
- **Mushrooms**: If using dried mushrooms, make sure to rehydrate them well to achieve a similar texture to fresh mushrooms.
- **Flavor**: Adjust the sweetness and saltiness of the sauce to your taste by varying the amount of sugar and soy sauce.

Braised Chicken with Shiitake Mushrooms is a hearty and savory dish that brings together the umami-rich flavor of shiitake mushrooms with tender chicken. It's a great option for a satisfying dinner that's easy to prepare and packed with flavor. Enjoy this comforting meal!

Japanese Style Stuffed Peppers

Ingredients:

- **For the Stuffed Peppers**:
    - 4 large bell peppers (any color)
    - 1/2 lb (225 g) ground pork or ground chicken
    - 1 cup cooked white or short-grain rice (cooled)
    - 1/4 cup onion, finely chopped
    - 1 clove garlic, minced
    - 1 tablespoon soy sauce
    - 1 tablespoon mirin (or dry white wine)
    - 1 teaspoon sesame oil
    - 1 teaspoon grated ginger
    - 1/2 teaspoon salt
    - 1/4 teaspoon black pepper
    - 1/4 cup chopped fresh parsley or green onions (for garnish, optional)
- **For the Sauce**:
    - 1 cup tomato sauce
    - 1 tablespoon soy sauce
    - 1 tablespoon sugar (or honey)
    - 1 tablespoon rice vinegar
    - 1 teaspoon sesame oil

Instructions:

1. **Prepare the Bell Peppers**:
    1. **Cut and Clean Peppers**: Cut the tops off the bell peppers and remove the seeds and membranes. Set aside.
2. **Prepare the Filling**:
    1. **Cook Aromatics**: In a large bowl, mix the ground meat, cooked rice, finely chopped onion, minced garlic, soy sauce, mirin, sesame oil, grated ginger, salt, and black pepper until well combined.
3. **Stuff the Peppers**:
    1. **Fill Peppers**: Stuff each bell pepper with the meat and rice mixture, packing it in firmly.
4. **Prepare the Sauce**:
    1. **Mix Sauce Ingredients**: In a small bowl, combine the tomato sauce, soy sauce, sugar (or honey), rice vinegar, and sesame oil. Stir well.
5. **Cook the Stuffed Peppers**:
    1. **Simmer**: Place the stuffed peppers in a large skillet or pot. Pour the sauce over the peppers.

2. **Cover and Cook**: Cover the skillet or pot and simmer over medium-low heat for about 20-30 minutes, or until the peppers are tender and the filling is cooked through. You can occasionally spoon some sauce over the tops of the peppers during cooking.
6. **Finish and Serve**:
    1. **Garnish**: Once cooked, remove the peppers from the pot and place them on serving plates. Spoon some of the sauce from the skillet over the peppers.
    2. **Garnish**: Garnish with chopped fresh parsley or green onions if desired.
    3. **Serve**: Serve hot, either on its own or with steamed rice.

Tips:

- **Meat**: Ground pork or chicken works well, but you can also use ground beef or a mixture of meats.
- **Rice**: Make sure the rice is cooled before mixing it with the meat to avoid cooking the meat prematurely.
- **Sauce**: Adjust the sweetness or saltiness of the sauce according to your taste preference.

Japanese-Style Stuffed Peppers combine the hearty texture of stuffed peppers with the distinctive flavors of Japanese cuisine, offering a comforting and satisfying meal. Enjoy these flavorful stuffed peppers as a main dish or a hearty side!

Miso-Glazed Chicken Wings

Ingredients:

- **For the Chicken Wings**:
    - 2 lbs (900 g) chicken wings
    - 1 tablespoon vegetable oil (or sesame oil)
    - 2 tablespoons sesame seeds (optional, for garnish)
    - 2 green onions, sliced (optional, for garnish)
- **For the Miso Glaze**:
    - 1/4 cup white miso paste (or yellow miso)
    - 1/4 cup soy sauce
    - 1/4 cup mirin (or dry white wine)
    - 2 tablespoons sugar (or honey)
    - 1 tablespoon rice vinegar
    - 1 clove garlic, minced
    - 1 teaspoon grated ginger
    - 1 teaspoon sesame oil

Instructions:

1. **Prepare the Chicken Wings**:
    1. **Preheat Oven**: Preheat your oven to 400°F (200°C).
    2. **Dry Wings**: Pat the chicken wings dry with paper towels. This helps the skin get crispy.
    3. **Season**: Toss the wings with vegetable oil (or sesame oil) and season with a pinch of salt and pepper.
2. **Cook the Chicken Wings**:
    1. **Arrange on Baking Sheet**: Place the wings in a single layer on a baking sheet lined with parchment paper or a lightly oiled rack.
    2. **Bake**: Bake in the preheated oven for 25-30 minutes, or until the wings are golden brown and crispy, flipping them halfway through cooking.
3. **Prepare the Miso Glaze**:
    1. **Mix Glaze Ingredients**: In a medium bowl, whisk together the white miso paste, soy sauce, mirin, sugar (or honey), rice vinegar, minced garlic, grated ginger, and sesame oil until smooth and well combined.
4. **Glaze the Wings**:
    1. **Coat with Glaze**: Once the wings are cooked, remove them from the oven and brush them generously with the miso glaze.
    2. **Return to Oven**: Return the glazed wings to the oven and bake for an additional 5-10 minutes, or until the glaze is caramelized and sticky.
5. **Finish and Serve**:
    1. **Garnish**: Sprinkle with sesame seeds and sliced green onions if desired.

2. **Serve**: Serve the wings hot as an appetizer or main dish. They can be enjoyed on their own or with a side of steamed rice or vegetables.

Tips:

- **Glaze Thickness**: If the glaze is too thick, you can thin it with a little water or more mirin. If too thin, cook it down a bit longer on the stove until it reaches your desired consistency.
- **Grilling Option**: You can also grill the wings. Preheat your grill to medium-high heat and grill the wings, brushing with the miso glaze during the last few minutes of cooking.

Miso-Glazed Chicken Wings are a savory and slightly sweet treat with an irresistible umami flavor. They're perfect for entertaining or as a delicious everyday meal. Enjoy these flavorful wings with your favorite sides or as a stand-alone delight!

Hot and Sour Udon Soup

Ingredients:

- **For the Soup:**
    - 200 g (7 oz) udon noodles (fresh or dried)
    - 1 tablespoon vegetable oil (or sesame oil)
    - 1 cup shiitake mushrooms, sliced (or any preferred mushrooms)
    - 1 medium carrot, julienned
    - 1 bell pepper, sliced (red or green)
    - 1 cup baby spinach or bok choy
    - 2 cloves garlic, minced
    - 1-inch piece of ginger, minced
    - 4 cups chicken or vegetable broth
    - 2 tablespoons soy sauce
    - 1 tablespoon rice vinegar
    - 1 tablespoon chili paste (adjust to taste)
    - 1 tablespoon miso paste (optional, for extra umami)
    - 1 teaspoon sugar (or honey)
    - 1 teaspoon sesame oil (for finishing)
    - 1-2 teaspoons white pepper (adjust to taste)
    - 2 green onions, sliced (for garnish)
    - 1 tablespoon chopped cilantro (optional, for garnish)
    - 1 tablespoon sesame seeds (optional, for garnish)
- **For the Toppings (Optional):**
    - 1 soft-boiled egg (or poached egg)
    - Sliced bamboo shoots or water chestnuts
    - Pickled vegetables (e.g., kimchi or pickled radish)

Instructions:

1. **Prepare the Udon Noodles:**
    1. **Cook Noodles:** Cook the udon noodles according to the package instructions. Drain and set aside.
2. **Prepare the Soup Base:**
    1. **Heat Oil:** In a large pot, heat the vegetable oil over medium heat.
    2. **Sauté Aromatics:** Add the minced garlic and ginger. Sauté for 1-2 minutes until fragrant.
    3. **Add Vegetables:** Add the sliced mushrooms, carrot, and bell pepper to the pot. Cook for about 5 minutes until the vegetables begin to soften.
3. **Prepare the Broth:**
    1. **Add Broth:** Pour in the chicken or vegetable broth and bring to a boil.

2. **Add Seasonings**: Stir in the soy sauce, rice vinegar, chili paste, miso paste (if using), sugar, and white pepper. Reduce the heat and let the broth simmer for about 5-10 minutes to allow the flavors to meld.
4. **Add Greens and Noodles**:
    1. **Add Greens**: Stir in the baby spinach or bok choy and cook for 1-2 minutes until wilted.
    2. **Add Noodles**: Add the cooked udon noodles to the pot and stir to heat through.
5. **Finish and Serve**:
    1. **Adjust Seasoning**: Taste the soup and adjust the seasoning with additional soy sauce, vinegar, or chili paste if needed.
    2. **Finish with Sesame Oil**: Drizzle in the sesame oil and give the soup a final stir.
    3. **Garnish**: Serve the soup hot, garnished with sliced green onions, chopped cilantro, and sesame seeds if desired.
    4. **Add Toppings**: If using, add a soft-boiled egg, sliced bamboo shoots, or pickled vegetables on top.

Tips:

- **Heat Level**: Adjust the amount of chili paste to control the spiciness of the soup. You can start with less and add more to taste.
- **Broth**: For a richer flavor, you can use homemade broth or add a splash of sake or soy sauce.
- **Noodles**: Fresh udon noodles work best, but dried noodles can also be used. Adjust cooking time according to the package instructions.

Hot and Sour Udon Soup combines the comforting warmth of a noodle soup with a tangy and spicy kick, making it a delicious and satisfying dish. Enjoy this flavorful soup as a hearty meal or a comforting bowl on a chilly day!

Tempura Soba Noodles

Ingredients:

- **For the Soba Noodles:**
    - 200 g (7 oz) soba noodles (buckwheat noodles)
    - 1 tablespoon soy sauce
    - 1 tablespoon mirin (or dry white wine)
    - 1 tablespoon sake (optional)
    - 1 teaspoon sugar (or honey)
- **For the Tempura:**
    - 1 cup all-purpose flour
    - 1/2 cup cornstarch
    - 1 teaspoon baking powder
    - 1 large egg
    - 1 cup cold sparkling water (or ice-cold water)
    - 8-10 shrimp, peeled and deveined
    - 1 medium sweet potato, thinly sliced
    - 1 small zucchini, thinly sliced
    - 1 cup vegetable oil (for frying)
- **For the Broth:**
    - 4 cups dashi broth (or chicken/vegetable broth)
    - 2 tablespoons soy sauce
    - 1 tablespoon mirin
    - 1 teaspoon sugar (or honey)
    - 1 clove garlic, minced (optional)
    - 1 small piece of ginger, minced (optional)
- **Garnishes:**
    - 2 green onions, sliced
    - 1 tablespoon sesame seeds
    - Pickled ginger (optional)
    - Seaweed strips (nori or wakame) (optional)

Instructions:

1. **Prepare the Tempura:**
    - **Mix Tempura Batter:** In a bowl, whisk together the flour, cornstarch, and baking powder. Add the egg and cold sparkling water, stirring gently until just combined. The batter should be lumpy.
    - **Heat Oil:** Heat the vegetable oil in a deep pan or fryer to 350°F (175°C).
    - **Coat and Fry:** Dip the shrimp, sweet potato slices, and zucchini slices in the tempura batter, allowing excess batter to drip off. Fry in batches until golden and

crispy, about 2-3 minutes per piece. Remove with a slotted spoon and drain on paper towels.
2. **Cook the Soba Noodles**:
   - **Cook Noodles**: Bring a large pot of water to a boil. Cook the soba noodles according to the package instructions, usually about 4-5 minutes. Drain and rinse under cold water to stop the cooking process. Set aside.
3. **Prepare the Broth**:
   - **Combine Ingredients**: In a pot, combine the dashi broth, soy sauce, mirin, sugar, garlic, and ginger (if using). Bring to a simmer and cook for 5-10 minutes to meld the flavors. Adjust seasoning to taste.
4. **Assemble the Dish**:
   - **Heat Noodles**: Divide the soba noodles among serving bowls. Pour the hot broth over the noodles.
   - **Top with Tempura**: Arrange the tempura on top of the noodles and broth.
   - **Garnish**: Sprinkle with sliced green onions, sesame seeds, pickled ginger, and seaweed strips if desired.
5. **Serve**:
   - Serve the Tempura Soba Noodles hot, and enjoy the combination of the crispy tempura with the warm, savory broth and tender soba noodles.

Tips:

- **Tempura Batter**: Use cold sparkling water or ice-cold water for a light and crispy batter. Do not overmix; lumps in the batter are fine.
- **Broth**: Adjust the saltiness and sweetness of the broth to your taste by adding more soy sauce or sugar.
- **Noodles**: Rinse the soba noodles under cold water after cooking to prevent them from becoming sticky.

Tempura Soba Noodles is a perfect blend of textures and flavors, with the crunchy tempura complementing the nutty soba noodles and flavorful broth. It's a comforting and satisfying dish that's great for any time of year. Enjoy your delicious meal!

Korean-Style Spicy Tofu Stew

Ingredients:

- **For the Stew:**
    - 1 tablespoon vegetable oil (or sesame oil)
    - 1/2 onion, finely chopped
    - 2 cloves garlic, minced
    - 1 small piece of ginger, minced
    - 1-2 Korean red chili peppers (or 1-2 tablespoons Korean chili paste, gochujang)
    - 1 tablespoon Korean chili flakes (gochugaru) (adjust to taste)
    - 1 cup kimchi, chopped (optional, for added flavor)
    - 1 cup shiitake mushrooms, sliced (or other mushrooms)
    - 1 medium zucchini, sliced
    - 2 cups vegetable or chicken broth
    - 1 tablespoon soy sauce
    - 1 tablespoon fish sauce (optional, for depth of flavor)
    - 1 block soft or silken tofu (about 14 oz), cut into cubes
    - 1 teaspoon sesame oil (for finishing)
    - 2 green onions, sliced (for garnish)
    - 1 tablespoon chopped cilantro (optional, for garnish)
    - 1 egg (optional, for adding to the stew)

Instructions:

1. **Prepare the Base:**
    - **Heat Oil:** In a large pot or Korean earthenware pot (dolsot), heat the vegetable oil over medium heat.
    - **Sauté Aromatics:** Add the chopped onion, minced garlic, and minced ginger. Sauté for about 2-3 minutes until fragrant and the onion is translucent.
2. **Add Spices and Vegetables:**
    - **Add Spices:** Stir in the Korean red chili peppers (or gochujang), Korean chili flakes (gochugaru), and chopped kimchi (if using). Cook for another 2 minutes, allowing the spices to release their flavors.
    - **Add Vegetables:** Add the sliced mushrooms and zucchini. Cook for another 5 minutes, stirring occasionally.
3. **Make the Broth:**
    - **Add Broth:** Pour in the vegetable or chicken broth, soy sauce, and fish sauce (if using). Bring to a simmer and cook for about 5 minutes.
4. **Add Tofu and Simmer:**
    - **Add Tofu:** Gently add the cubed tofu to the pot. Be careful not to break up the tofu too much.

- **Simmer**: Let the stew simmer for an additional 5-10 minutes to allow the flavors to meld and the tofu to heat through.
5. **Finish and Serve**:
   - **Add Sesame Oil**: Drizzle the sesame oil over the stew and stir gently.
   - **Add Egg (Optional)**: If you're adding an egg, make a small well in the stew and crack the egg into the well. Cover the pot and let the egg poach for a few minutes until it reaches your desired level of doneness.
   - **Garnish**: Garnish with sliced green onions and chopped cilantro if desired.
6. **Serve**:
   - Serve the hot stew directly from the pot, with steamed rice on the side. Enjoy the rich, spicy flavors of this comforting dish!

Tips:

- **Tofu**: Use soft or silken tofu for the traditional texture. If you prefer a firmer texture, you can use medium or firm tofu, but be sure to cut it into larger cubes to prevent it from breaking apart.
- **Spice Level**: Adjust the amount of Korean chili flakes and chili paste to control the spiciness of the stew. Start with less and add more if you like it spicier.
- **Kimchi**: Adding kimchi enhances the flavor and provides an extra layer of complexity to the stew, but it's optional if you prefer a more straightforward flavor.

Korean-Style Spicy Tofu Stew is a flavorful and hearty dish that's perfect for a warming meal. The combination of spicy broth, tender tofu, and vegetables makes it a satisfying and comforting choice, especially on a cold day. Enjoy!

Sweet Potato and Pork Stew

Ingredients:

- **For the Stew:**
    - 1 lb (450 g) pork shoulder or pork belly, cut into bite-sized chunks
    - 2 tablespoons vegetable oil (or olive oil)
    - 1 medium onion, chopped
    - 2 cloves garlic, minced
    - 1-inch piece of ginger, minced
    - 2 medium sweet potatoes, peeled and cut into chunks
    - 2 medium carrots, peeled and sliced
    - 1 cup celery, sliced
    - 1 cup green beans, trimmed and cut into pieces
    - 4 cups chicken or vegetable broth
    - 1 tablespoon soy sauce
    - 1 tablespoon mirin (or dry white wine)
    - 1 tablespoon sugar (or honey)
    - 1 teaspoon ground black pepper
    - 1 teaspoon dried thyme (or rosemary)
    - 2 bay leaves
    - 1 tablespoon cornstarch mixed with 2 tablespoons water (for thickening, optional)
    - Salt to taste
- **For Garnish:**
    - Fresh parsley or cilantro, chopped
    - Freshly ground black pepper

Instructions:

1. **Prepare the Pork:**
    1. Brown Pork: Heat the vegetable oil in a large pot or Dutch oven over medium-high heat. Add the pork chunks and cook until browned on all sides, about 5-7 minutes. Remove the pork from the pot and set aside.
2. **Prepare the Base:**
    1. Sauté Aromatics: In the same pot, add the chopped onion, minced garlic, and minced ginger. Sauté for 2-3 minutes until fragrant and the onion is translucent.
3. **Build the Stew:**
    1. Add Vegetables: Return the browned pork to the pot. Add the sweet potatoes, carrots, celery, and green beans. Stir to combine.
    2. Add Liquid: Pour in the chicken or vegetable broth, soy sauce, mirin, sugar, ground black pepper, dried thyme (or rosemary), and bay leaves. Stir well.

3. Simmer: Bring the stew to a boil, then reduce the heat to low. Cover and let it simmer for 30-40 minutes, or until the pork is tender and the vegetables are cooked through.

4. **Thicken the Stew (Optional):**
   1. Add Cornstarch Mixture: If you prefer a thicker stew, stir in the cornstarch mixture and cook for an additional 5 minutes, or until the stew has thickened to your liking.

5. **Season and Serve:**
   1. Adjust Seasoning: Taste the stew and adjust the seasoning with salt and additional black pepper if needed.
   2. Garnish: Serve the stew hot, garnished with fresh parsley or cilantro and freshly ground black pepper.

Tips:

- Pork: Pork shoulder works well because it becomes tender and flavorful as it cooks. Pork belly adds extra richness if you prefer a fattier option.
- Sweet Potatoes: Cut the sweet potatoes into uniform chunks to ensure even cooking. You can use orange or purple sweet potatoes.
- Thickening: If you prefer a thicker stew without using cornstarch, you can mash some of the sweet potatoes in the stew with a fork to naturally thicken it.

Sweet Potato and Pork Stew is a comforting and flavorful dish that combines the sweetness of sweet potatoes with the heartiness of pork. It's perfect for a satisfying dinner, especially when served with a side of crusty bread or over rice. Enjoy!

Get smarter responses, upload files and images, and more.

Miso Cod Fish

Ingredients:

- **For the Miso Marinade**:
    - 1/4 cup white miso paste
    - 2 tablespoons mirin (sweet rice wine)
    - 2 tablespoons sake (or dry white wine)
    - 2 tablespoons sugar (or honey)
    - 1 tablespoon soy sauce
    - 1 teaspoon grated ginger (optional)
    - 1 teaspoon sesame oil (optional)
- **For the Cod**:
    - 4 cod fillets (about 6 oz each), skinless
    - Salt, for seasoning
- **For Garnish**:
    - Sliced green onions
    - Sesame seeds
    - Lemon wedges (optional)

Instructions:

1. **Prepare the Miso Marinade**:
    1. **Combine Ingredients**: In a bowl, whisk together the white miso paste, mirin, sake, sugar, soy sauce, grated ginger, and sesame oil until smooth and well combined.
2. **Marinate the Cod**:
    1. **Season Cod**: Pat the cod fillets dry with paper towels and season lightly with salt.
    2. **Apply Marinade**: Place the cod fillets in a resealable plastic bag or shallow dish. Spread the miso marinade evenly over the fish, ensuring each fillet is well-coated. Seal the bag or cover the dish.
    3. **Refrigerate**: Marinate the cod in the refrigerator for at least 30 minutes, or up to 2 hours for a more intense flavor. Avoid marinating for too long as the miso can overpower the delicate flavor of the cod.
3. **Cook the Cod**:
    1. **Preheat Oven/Broiler**: Preheat your oven to 400°F (200°C) or set your broiler to high.
    2. **Prepare Baking Sheet**: Line a baking sheet with parchment paper or lightly grease it.
    3. **Bake/Broil**: Remove the cod fillets from the marinade and place them on the prepared baking sheet. Bake in the preheated oven for about 12-15 minutes, or

broil for 4-6 minutes, until the fish is opaque and flakes easily with a fork. The top should be caramelized and slightly crispy.
4. **Garnish and Serve**:
    1. **Garnish**: Transfer the cooked cod fillets to serving plates. Garnish with sliced green onions and sesame seeds.
    2. **Serve**: Serve the miso cod fish hot, with lemon wedges on the side if desired. It pairs well with steamed rice, sautéed vegetables, or a fresh salad.

Tips:

- **Marinade**: Adjust the sweetness or saltiness of the marinade to your taste by adding more sugar or soy sauce if needed.
- **Cooking Method**: Broiling gives the cod a nicely caramelized top, while baking is a more gentle method. Both methods work well, so choose based on your preference.
- **Miso Paste**: White miso is preferred for its mild flavor, but you can also use red miso for a stronger flavor if desired.

Miso Cod Fish is a flavorful and sophisticated dish that is both easy to prepare and impressive enough for a special occasion. The miso marinade imparts a rich umami flavor, making the cod tender and delicious. Enjoy!

Niku Jaga (Beef and Potato Stew)

Ingredients:

- **For the Stew:**
    - 1 lb (450 g) beef sirloin or ribeye, thinly sliced into bite-sized pieces
    - 2 tablespoons vegetable oil (or sesame oil)
    - 1 large onion, sliced
    - 2 medium potatoes, peeled and cut into chunks
    - 1 medium carrot, peeled and sliced
    - 1 cup green beans, trimmed and cut into pieces (optional)
    - 1 cup dashi broth (or beef or vegetable broth)
    - 3 tablespoons soy sauce
    - 2 tablespoons mirin (sweet rice wine)
    - 2 tablespoons sugar (or honey)
    - 1 tablespoon sake (optional, or dry white wine)
    - 1 teaspoon salt (adjust to taste)
    - 1 teaspoon ground black pepper (optional)
- **For Garnish:**
    - Sliced green onions
    - Sesame seeds (optional)

Instructions:

1. **Prepare the Ingredients:**
    - **Cut Beef:** Slice the beef into bite-sized pieces.
    - **Prepare Vegetables:** Peel and cut the potatoes into chunks. Slice the onion and carrot. Trim and cut the green beans if using.
2. **Sauté the Beef:**
    - **Heat Oil:** In a large pot or Dutch oven, heat the vegetable oil over medium-high heat.
    - **Cook Beef:** Add the beef slices and cook until browned on all sides, about 3-4 minutes. Remove the beef from the pot and set aside.
3. **Cook the Vegetables:**
    - **Sauté Onions:** In the same pot, add the sliced onion and cook until softened and slightly caramelized, about 5 minutes.
    - **Add Carrots and Potatoes:** Add the carrot and potato chunks to the pot and cook for an additional 3-4 minutes, stirring occasionally.
4. **Make the Stew:**
    - **Combine Ingredients:** Return the browned beef to the pot. Add the dashi broth, soy sauce, mirin, sugar, and sake (if using). Stir to combine.

- **Simmer**: Bring the mixture to a boil, then reduce the heat to low. Cover and let it simmer for about 20-25 minutes, or until the potatoes and carrots are tender and the flavors are well combined.
5. **Finish the Dish**:
    - **Add Green Beans**: If using green beans, add them to the pot during the last 5 minutes of cooking.
    - **Season**: Taste the stew and adjust seasoning with salt and pepper as needed.
6. **Serve**:
    - Serve the **Niku Jaga** hot, garnished with sliced green onions and sesame seeds if desired. It pairs wonderfully with steamed rice.

Tips:

- **Beef**: Use well-marbled beef for the best flavor and tenderness. Thinly sliced beef is traditional, but you can also use thicker cuts if preferred.
- **Potatoes**: Waxy potatoes like Yukon Gold or red potatoes work well because they hold their shape better during cooking.
- **Sweetness and Saltiness**: Adjust the sugar and soy sauce to suit your taste preferences. You can add more sugar for a sweeter flavor or more soy sauce for added saltiness.

Niku Jaga is a comforting, flavorful dish that is perfect for a family meal. The combination of tender beef, hearty potatoes, and sweet-savory sauce makes it a dish that is both satisfying and heartwarming. Enjoy!

Spicy Tuna Pizza

Ingredients:

- **For the Pizza:**
    - 1 pizza dough (store-bought or homemade)
    - 1 cup shredded mozzarella cheese
    - 1/2 cup mayonnaise
    - 2 tablespoons Sriracha or another hot sauce (adjust to taste)
    - 1 can (5 oz) tuna, drained and flaked
    - 1/4 cup finely chopped red onion
    - 1/4 cup finely chopped celery
    - 1/4 cup chopped cucumber
    - 1 tablespoon soy sauce
    - 1 tablespoon sesame oil
    - 1 tablespoon chopped fresh cilantro (for garnish)
- **For the Toppings:**
    - 1/2 avocado, sliced
    - 1/4 cup sliced green onions
    - 1 tablespoon sesame seeds (optional)
    - Pickled ginger (for serving, optional)
    - Soy sauce (for drizzling, optional)

Instructions:

1. **Prepare the Oven and Dough:**
    - **Preheat Oven:** Preheat your oven to 475°F (245°C). If using a pizza stone, place it in the oven to heat up.
    - **Roll Out Dough:** On a floured surface, roll out the pizza dough to your desired thickness and shape. Transfer it to a pizza peel or a baking sheet lined with parchment paper.
2. **Prepare the Spicy Tuna Mixture:**
    - **Mix Ingredients:** In a bowl, combine the mayonnaise, Sriracha (or hot sauce), and soy sauce. Stir well.
    - **Add Tuna:** Fold in the flaked tuna, finely chopped red onion, celery, and cucumber until well combined.
    - **Season:** Add the sesame oil and mix again. Adjust seasoning with additional Sriracha or soy sauce if needed.
3. **Assemble the Pizza:**
    - **Add Cheese:** Spread a layer of shredded mozzarella cheese evenly over the pizza dough.
    - **Top with Tuna Mixture:** Spoon the spicy tuna mixture over the cheese, spreading it out evenly.

4. **Bake the Pizza**:
    - **Bake**: Place the pizza in the preheated oven on the baking sheet or pizza stone. Bake for 10-12 minutes, or until the crust is golden brown and the cheese is melted and bubbly.
5. **Add Fresh Toppings**:
    - **Garnish**: Once the pizza is out of the oven, top with sliced avocado, sliced green onions, and sesame seeds if using.
    - **Serve**: Garnish with chopped fresh cilantro. Optionally, serve with pickled ginger and a drizzle of soy sauce.
6. **Cut and Enjoy**:
    - Slice the pizza into wedges and serve hot.

Tips:

- **Dough**: If you prefer a crispier crust, pre-bake the dough for 5 minutes before adding the toppings.
- **Spice Level**: Adjust the amount of Sriracha or hot sauce according to your preference for spiciness.
- **Toppings**: You can customize the pizza with additional toppings such as thinly sliced radishes or jalapeños for extra flavor and crunch.

Spicy Tuna Pizza is a fun and inventive way to enjoy the flavors of sushi in a pizza format. The combination of spicy tuna, creamy avocado, and melted cheese creates a unique and satisfying dish that's perfect for a casual meal or entertaining guests. Enjoy!

www.ingramcontent.com/pod-product-compliance
Lightning Source LLC
LaVergne TN
LVHW081600060526
838201LV00054B/1995